AF668735

Broken to Built

How GOD Restores Lives, Heals Hearts & Uses Broken People for HIS Glory

Gerard Assey

Broken to Built:
How GOD Restores Lives, Heals Hearts & Uses Broken People for HIS Glory

By

Gerard Assey

Published by:
Gerard Assey
19/18, Palli Arasan Street
Anna Nagar East
Chennai - 600 102

ISBN: 978-81-995134-7-1

Table of Contents

Preface

There are moments in life when something breaks so deeply within us that we wonder if anything good can ever come out of the shattered pieces. For many years, I believed brokenness was a problem to hide, a flaw to fix, or a wound to forget. But God, in His gentle mercy, began to show me that brokenness was not the end of the story—it was the doorway to His greatest work.

This book: **"Broken to Built: *How GOD Restores Lives, Heals Hearts & Uses Broken People for HIS Glory"*** was born not in a study room, but in the workshop of life. It began with old transistor radios, damaged furniture, and burnt guitars rescued from garbage bins. It grew as I sat with abused wives, wounded husbands, abandoned children, addicts, and weary souls in a little home church near a slum. It deepened as I watched God breathe life back into those the world had written off. And it matured as I realized that the same God who restored objects in my hands was restoring hearts in His hands—including my own.

Every chapter in this book carries a simple, unchanging truth:

- ✓ ***What is surrendered to God is never wasted.***
- ✓ ***What is laid before Him is never lost.***
- ✓ ***What is broken in His hands becomes a masterpiece in His timing.***

If you are holding this book, perhaps you are carrying wounds no one sees. Or maybe you are a pastor, counselor, teacher, parent, or friend walking beside someone whose heart has been shattered. Wherever you stand, my prayer is that these pages become a gentle companion on your journey—a voice of hope, a reminder of grace, and a witness to the God who never discards what is damaged.

The One who shaped galaxies and stars also shapes scars.

The One who healed nations still heals individuals.

The One who restored kings still restores ordinary people like us.

May you feel His nearness as you read.

May you see His hand in your story.

And may you rise from these pages knowing you are not simply repaired— **you are being rebuilt for His glory!**

Welcome to the journey from **Broken to Built**.

A journey only God can finish.

The Day I Learned to Love the Broken

I never planned to love broken things. Neither did I set out to love broken people. Yet looking back, I realize that much of my life has been God patiently shaping my heart—sometimes quietly, sometimes through frustration, and many times through unexpected lessons—until I finally understood that He had been teaching me to see value where others saw none.

Even as a young boy, I had a strange fascination with old, used, discarded items. While other children my age were drawn to shiny new things, I found myself wandering into second-hand shops—those dusty little rooms stacked with forgotten radios, half-working typewriters, transistor parts, cassette players with knobs missing, broken guitar pickups, and furniture that seemed tired of standing upright. Most people walked past these items without a second look. But something in me always whispered, *"Look again… there's still life in this."*

I would purchase these items for next to nothing, bring them home, and sit for hours examining wires, cleaning rust, tightening screws, and slowly watching something useless take shape again. Many years later, I realized that what I felt was not simply excitement—it was a quiet joy, a tender delight in the possibility of restoration. I loved watching something that had once failed, once fallen, once been written off—come back to life. I didn't know it then, but God was shaping my heart to recognize the same potential in people.

From as early as I can remember, something in me was drawn to anything wounded or fragile. One of my earliest memories is from when I was about five years old. I saw a tiny sparrow that had been knocked down, its leg twisted and broken. While the adults around me simply walked past, something in my little heart could not. I picked it up gently, held it close, and carried it home as if it were the most precious thing in the world. I remember sitting on the floor, determined to heal it, pressing its broken leg into place and wrapping it carefully with cello tape—the only "medical equipment" I knew at that age. Everyone burst out laughing at the sight. Years later, even when my own children were born, my parents continued to retell that story—how a small boy genuinely believed he could fix a broken sparrow with tape and tenderness. What I did not know then was that God was already planting in me a heart that could not walk away from brokenness. Even in childish innocence, He was shaping in me the instinct to pick up what others overlook.

As adulthood came and life became busy—with a career, responsibilities, marriage, children, and the daily race of living—my hobby disappeared into the background. I didn't have time for broken things anymore. Or so I thought. But God has a way of bringing back into focus what He planted in us long before we understood its purpose.

A Refrigerator, a Wire, and a Whisper From God

Many years later, after our children had grown and begun their own families, we were left with the quiet rhythm of an older home—until one morning, our 17-year-old refrigerator stopped working. My wife was convinced that this was the end. "It's done. Let's buy a new one today itself," she insisted.

The technician who came examined it for a few minutes and declared with absolute certainty, *"The compressor is dead. This model is outdated. It's better to buy a new fridge."*

My wife nodded; I hesitated. Something inside me refused to give up so quickly. I told her, *"Give me a few hours. Let me at least take a look."*

Almost instinctively, the old curiosity resurfaced. I called a friend who knew about appliances, and together we opened the back panel. We checked each connection slowly, carefully. After a few minutes, he pointed to a single wire—thin, slightly melted, broken at a point so small you would miss it if you weren't looking for it.

"This is your problem," he said. A wire costing just a few rupees. We replaced it. The fridge hummed back to life. That was over a year and a half ago—and it still works perfectly today.

As I watched it come alive, I felt the Holy Spirit whisper, *"This is how many lives look from the outside—written off, declared dead, condemned as too old, too damaged, too far gone. But sometimes, all they need is one connection restored—one touch, one prayer, one moment of care—for life to return."*

That day, God reminded me that nothing is too broken for Him to repair.

Three Burnt Guitars and a Lesson I Did Not Expect

Sometime later, I was dropping my grandson Jonathan to his music class. As I waited outside, my eyes fell on a heap of charred, broken wood near the shop's garbage bin. Curious, I walked closer.

Jonathan followed reluctantly, probably embarrassed at the thought of his grandfather digging through a dustbin.

Inside the heap were the remains of three guitars—burnt, blackened, broken into nearly eight different pieces each. Their necks snapped, their bodies warped, their electronics melted. Anyone else would have stepped over them. But something in me—something old, something familiar—made me reach down and pick up the pieces.

My grandson looked horrified. To him, it was junk. To me, it felt like a divine appointment.

At first, I thought I would just salvage a few parts and restore them as decorative pieces. But as I began to work on them at home, cleaning, sanding, joining, repainting, replacing a few components—something remarkable happened. Slowly, each guitar began to take shape again. Each one began to sing again.

And then came the greatest surprise: one of the guitars, after careful scraping of the burnt label, turned out to be a high-end brand worth several thousands. Someone had thrown away a treasure because it looked beyond repair.

God spoke again. *"Many of My children look like these burnt guitars. Life's fires have charred them. Circumstances have broken them. People have thrown them aside. But I see the value in them. I see My design beneath the ashes."*

In that moment, I realized I was not simply restoring guitars—I was understanding God.

The Slum Church and the People God Sent to Me

Around the same season, I started a small home church. Most who attended came from a nearby slum—families struggling with addiction, violence, neglect, and poverty. Many were women who arrived with bruises—physical and emotional—carrying stories of alcoholic husbands, broken dreams, wandering children, and daily survival.

One woman, *Meera*, came every week with tears in her eyes. Her husband, lost in drunkenness, beat her almost daily. But every week she also returned with a testimony—*"Pastor, this week he came home a little earlier… this week he didn't shout at the children… this week he agreed to pray."* God was not mending her life in one dramatic moment—He was slowly reworking the broken wires, restoring one connection at a time.

Another man, *Rajan*, a young father trapped in drug addiction, sat outside during the first few meetings, unwilling to come in. But something kept drawing him. One day he walked into the service trembling. He wept throughout. That day, he met Jesus—not in a sermon, but in a moment of surrender. Today, he works as a delivery driver, supporting his family faithfully.

Week after week, our small home church became a workshop of restoration—a place where God gently, patiently, lovingly rebuilt lives others had written off.

I did not realize it then, but God was sculpting my calling. Just as I had restored old radios and broken guitars, He was now using me to partner with Him in restoring broken people.

The Ancient Art That Explains God's Heart

There is a Japanese art called Kintsugi, meaning "golden joinery." When a piece of pottery breaks, it is not thrown away. Instead, it is repaired with lacquer mixed with pure gold. The cracks are not hidden—they are highlighted. Not disguised—they are celebrated. What was broken becomes more beautiful and more valuable than before.

Kintsugi teaches one simple truth: brokenness does not reduce worth—it reveals it.

And isn't that exactly what God does?

Psalm 147:3 says,

"He heals the brokenhearted and binds up their wounds."

And Isaiah 57:15 reveals God's dwelling place:

"I live… with the one who is contrite and humble, to revive the spirit of the lowly."

God is attracted to brokenness.

He moves toward the cracks, not away from them.

He fills them, not with shame, but with His glory.

God's Pattern: Restoring the Broken Throughout Scripture

When I look at the broken people I've met, I'm reminded of many in Scripture who were shattered yet chosen.

In the Old Testament, Hannah was broken by barrenness and ridicule—but God turned her tears into Samuel, one of Israel's greatest prophets.

David was broken by failure, guilt, and sin—yet God called him "a man after My own heart." Joseph was broken by betrayal and imprisonment—yet God used the pieces to build a nation.

In the New Testament, Peter was broken by denial—yet Jesus restored him and built the early church through him. Mary Magdalene was broken by torment—yet she became the first to witness the risen Christ. Paul was broken by pride and blinded on the Damascus road—yet he became the apostle of grace.

Every story in Scripture reveals the same truth: God never discards the broken. He rebuilds them. He re-commissions them. He re-assigns them with greater purpose.

Brokenness Looks Different in Every Life

I once counseled a young man named *Aarav*, a successful professional who looked confident on the outside but was crumbling inside from the pressure to perform. His brokenness was invisible—but real.

Another woman, *Lydia*, was shattered by the memory of childhood abuse. Her life felt like a pile of fragmented emotions she didn't know how to glue together. But as she encountered God's healing love week after week, she slowly began to believe, *"Maybe God can make something beautiful out of this."*

Brokenness comes in many forms—some visible, some hidden. But in every case, God's response is the same: *He draws near. He revives. He rebuilds.*

Looking Back — And Looking Forward

As I look back today, I see a clear pattern in my life—a divine training I never recognized at the time.

- ✓ A little boy trying to set back the leg of a bird,
- ✓ A boy drawn to broken radios.
- ✓ A man repairing a refrigerator with one small wire.
- ✓ Three burnt guitars reborn into beautiful instruments.
- ✓ A small slum church filled with wounded people finding hope.

A string of experiences that finally revealed God's whisper: *"I am the God who restores.*
What others reject, I redeem.

What life breaks, I rebuild.
What the world throws away, I make into a masterpiece. And I am calling you to partner with Me in this work."

This book is not written by someone who studied brokenness from a distance, but by someone who has tasted its depth, witnessed its pain, and seen firsthand the miraculous beauty of God's restoration.
If you are broken, this book is for you.
If you love someone who is broken, this book is for you.
If you minister to the broken, this book is for you.
If you've ever wondered whether God can rebuild what life has shattered, this book is for you.
Because I have learned—again and again—that in God's hands, broken pieces are not wasted. They are the beginning of a masterpiece.

Understanding Brokenness: What It Is and What It Is Not

Brokenness is a word that often carries the scent of shame. For many, it feels like an admission of defeat—a sign that life has gone off the rails, that something inside us has malfunctioned, or that somehow we've disappointed God. People avoid using the word because it exposes vulnerability. It strips away the polished image we want others to believe. It reveals the parts of us we've spent years trying to hide.

And yet, in Scripture—and in life—brokenness is one of the most sacred places a person can stand.

Many misunderstand brokenness. They assume it means they are failures. They assume it means God is punishing them. They assume it means they are unusable, unworthy, and unwanted. But the truth is far more beautiful. Brokenness, in God's eyes, is not destruction—it is invitation. It is not the end of usefulness—it is the beginning of purpose. And it is not punishment—it is preparation for deeper fellowship with Him.

To understand what brokenness really is, we must first understand what it is not.

Brokenness Is Not Failure

One of the greatest deceptions people believe is that their brokenness means they have failed—failed God, failed their family, failed spiritually, failed morally, or failed in life. But if brokenness were an indicator of failure, then some of Scripture's greatest heroes would be disqualified.

Job was a righteous man—"blameless and upright" as the Scripture says (Job 1:1). Yet he walked through a season so crushing that even his closest friends concluded, "Surely you have sinned." His wife, overwhelmed by grief, told him to "curse God and die." But Job's brokenness was not the result of failure—it was the place where the depth of his trust in God was revealed. And in the end, Job could say something few could: "My ears had heard of You, but now my eyes have seen You" (Job 42:5). He did not fail—he discovered God more intimately.

David, too, walked through seasons of deep brokenness—not only because of his own sin, but also because of betrayal, loss, persecution, and internal conflict. The man who defeated Goliath was also the man who cried out, "I am poured out like water" (Psalm 22:14). His brokenness did not disqualify him. It made him the man "after God's own heart."

I once met a young entrepreneur named *Rohit*, who lost his entire business due to an unexpected economic downturn. Everything he built collapsed in one year, and he walked into my office with tears running down his face. "I've failed God," he whispered. "If I were truly blessed, this wouldn't have happened."

But as he unfolded his story, it became obvious that his season of brokenness wasn't about failure—it was about refining. He had built his company on exhaustion, self-dependence, and endless striving. His identity had merged with his achievements. It took the collapse for him to discover who he was without the applause. When he surrendered his plans, God opened doors he could never have imagined. Today, he runs a mentoring network helping young business owners avoid the same pitfalls.

Sometimes what feels like failure is actually God's way of rearranging our priorities, repositioning us, and rebuilding our foundations.

Brokenness Is Not Punishment

Many also assume that brokenness must be God's way of paying them back for past sins or failures. This assumption comes from a distorted understanding of God's heart. Scripture repeatedly reveals that God is compassionate toward the broken, not harsh.

"*The Lord is close to the brokenhearted and saves those who are crushed in spirit.*" Psalm 34:18

"*I dwell… with the one who is contrite and humble.*"- Isaiah 57:15

Punishment is meant to harm. Brokenness, however, draws God nearer.

Consider Moses. He was raised in a palace, groomed for leadership, full of passion—but also full of untempered anger. When he struck the Egyptian and fled into the desert, Moses experienced forty years of what many would call "punishment," a life stripped down to nothing. But what seemed like exile was really preparation. God was not punishing Moses. He was shaping him. The man who once relied on his influence and education learned to rely on God alone.

The same pattern appears in the life of Paul. Before encountering Christ, Paul—then Saul—was proud, powerful, and deeply convinced he was right. His conversion left him blind for three days. Some might interpret this as punishment, but it was anything but that. God was breaking the arrogance that made

Paul spiritually blind long before his physical eyes failed. The temporary blindness allowed him to truly see.

I remember counseling a woman named *Shalini*, whose marriage had fallen apart after years of emotional neglect. She looked at her broken marriage and whispered, "This must be God punishing me for my past." But as she told her story, it became clear that her suffering was not divine retribution—it was the result of human choices, wounds, and unresolved pain.

I gently reminded her, "God does not punish you through the cruelty of others. Their choices were theirs. God's action is not to condemn you, but to heal what they damaged."

Over time, she rediscovered her identity, regained confidence, and even began helping other women who struggled with the same issues. Her brokenness was not punishment—it was the doorway to healing.

God's heart is never to destroy us. Rather, He breaks only what keeps us bound, never what keeps us close.

Brokenness Is Surrender, Honesty, and Exposure

If brokenness is not failure and not punishment, then what is it?

Brokenness is the place where all masks fall away. The place where we stop pretending. The place where we come to the end of our self-sufficiency. It is the moment when our strength is exhausted, our strategies don't work anymore, and our carefully constructed walls crack open. Brokenness is not the destruction of identity—it is the dismantling of illusions.

When David cried out in Psalm 51 after his sin with Bathsheba, he didn't bring excuses or explanations. He brought honesty. "*You desire truth in the inward parts*," he prayed (Psalm 51:6). His brokenness was the birthplace of repentance, renewal, and deeper intimacy with God.

In the New Testament, Peter epitomizes this truth. Though he pledged unwavering loyalty to Jesus, he denied Him three times—something he never imagined he was capable of. When the rooster crowed and Peter locked eyes with Jesus, Scripture says he "went out and wept bitterly" (Luke 22:62). His tears were not evidence of weakness, but of surrender.

And what did Jesus do? He didn't shame Peter. He restored him gently: "*Peter, do you love Me?*" "*Feed My sheep.*" Peter's brokenness became the platform for his ministry.

I once met a man named *Samir*, a successful musician who carried himself with confidence on stage but battled deep addictions off stage. For years he hid his struggles, convinced that admitting them would destroy his reputation. But after a near-collapse, he finally confessed, *"I can't keep this together anymore. I'm tired of pretending."*

His honesty became his turning point. In his brokenness, he surrendered his image, his secrets, and his fear. Slowly, God rebuilt his heart. Today, Samir leads worship with authenticity, helping others find freedom through transparency. His brokenness made him real—and God always works powerfully with what is real.

Brokenness is simply this: the place where God becomes our only strength because we finally admit our own weakness. When we surrender, we make room for God to work. When we become honest, healing begins. And when we allow God to expose what is hidden, He can finally restore what is hurting.

Brokenness Is the Beginning, Not the End

Brokenness may feel like collapse, but in God's hands it is transformation. It may feel like darkness, but it is actually the moment when God begins His deepest work. Job emerged with revelation. David emerged with a renewed heart. Moses emerged with divine authority. Paul emerged with purpose. Peter emerged with compassion and boldness.

Each of them discovered a truth that still holds today: God does not use the unbroken. He uses those who allow Him to break what is proud, stubborn, self-reliant, or hidden—so that grace may take over.

For individuals reading this, know this: your brokenness is not proof that God has abandoned you; it is proof that He is drawing near.

For counselors and pastors, remember that broken people do not need fixing—they need understanding, patience, and a gentle hand that leads them toward the Healer.

Brokenness is not a verdict. It is a process.

It is not a label. It is an invitation.

It is not an end. It is the beginning of being rebuilt by the One who makes all things new.

And in God's workshop, the broken are not thrown away. They are the very ones chosen for transformation.

Why God Allows Brokenness

There are seasons in life when the question surfaces from the depths of our soul, often whispered with trembling lips: *"If God loves me, why would He allow this?"*

It is a question pastors hear, counselors wrestle with, and ordinary believers ask in their darkest nights. And while no human answer can fully embrace the mystery of God's ways, Scripture gives us glimpses—windows into His heart, hints of His purposes, reminders of His sovereignty.

To understand brokenness, we must begin by understanding God.

The God Whose Ways Are Higher

Isaiah 55:8–9 offers a gentle but firm reminder: *"My thoughts are not your thoughts, neither are your ways My ways… As the heavens are higher than the earth, so are My ways higher than your ways."*

This is not God distancing Himself from our pain; it is God inviting us to trust Him in it. If an infant cannot understand a surgeon's hands, if a seed cannot understand why it must be buried, if gold cannot understand the heat of the fire—how much more difficult is it for finite hearts to grasp the intentions of an infinite God?

Yet this we know: God is sovereign, and His sovereignty is never cruel. Even when life breaks us, He remains good.

Brokenness is not God's pleasure, but it is often His pathway—His means of drawing us into deeper dependence, deeper maturity, deeper intimacy, and deeper purpose.

God allows what He could prevent.
But He prevents what would ultimately destroy us.
And He uses what He allows to refine us.

Three Sources of Pain—One Sovereign God

When people walk through painful seasons, they often assume that God is the direct cause. But Scripture paints a more nuanced picture.

- ✓ *Sometimes Satan attacks.*
- ✓ *Sometimes people wound us.*
- ✓ *Sometimes life simply happens in a fallen world.*

But God overrules every source and brings purpose out of the ruins.

Consider Joseph. His brothers hated him. Their jealousy drove them to strip him, betray him, and sell him into slavery. Potiphar's wife falsely accused him. The prison system forgot him. Human evil, false accusation, and injustice surrounded him for years.

Yet when Joseph finally faced his brothers, he didn't say, "Look what you did to me." Instead, he spoke the words only a restored heart could speak:

"You meant evil against me, but God meant it for good…" (Genesis 50:20).

He did not deny the evil.
He did not excuse it.
He did not pretend it didn't hurt.
But he recognized something deeper:
God can weave purpose even through human cruelty.
That does not make the cruelty good.
But it does mean that God never wastes the pain others cause.

When Satan Attacks

There are seasons in which the enemy targets our identity, our faith, or our destiny. This does not mean God abandons us; in fact, Scripture shows the opposite.

Satan sifted Peter.

He pursued Job.

He opposed Paul.

But in each case, God set the boundary, and His purpose prevailed.

Job's suffering was deep—far deeper than most of us will ever understand. His livestock, livelihood, health, reputation, and even his children were taken from him. Yet Scripture makes it clear:

Satan struck Job—but God sustained him.

Job's brokenness did not originate from God's cruelty; it was allowed under God's sovereignty. And through it, Job discovered a revelation of God he could never have known in a comfortable life.

In the New Testament, Jesus warned Peter, *"Satan has asked to sift you like wheat"* (Luke 22:31). But Jesus did not stop there. He continued: *"But I have prayed for you… and when you turn back, strengthen your brothers."*

Satan's attack was not the end; it was preparation. Peter's brokenness through failure became the foundation of his compassion as a shepherd.

When People Cause Pain

Brokenness is also born through the actions of people—betrayal, rejection, abandonment, disappointment, or injustice.

Moses fled Egypt not because God punished him, but because of fear, anger, rejection, and misunderstanding.

David was hunted by King Saul out of jealousy.
Paul was imprisoned because of religious hatred.
Jesus Himself was crucified because of human sin.
Yet in every case, God turned human cruelty into divine purpose.

I think of a woman I once counseled—let's call her *Anita*. She had been abandoned by her husband without warning, left to raise two children alone. The pain was unbearable, and she came to me weeping, asking, "*Why would God do this to me?*"

I held her hand and said, *"God didn't do this. A person made a sinful choice. But if you allow Him, God will heal you through this."*

And He did. Slowly, Anita rediscovered her strength, rebuilt her life, and eventually began to mentor single mothers in her church. What began as betrayal became a mantle of compassion.

Brokenness becomes redemptive when placed in God's hands.

People may cause pain—but only God can turn pain into purpose.

When Life Simply Happens

Sometimes brokenness comes simply because we live in a fallen world—illness, accidents, sudden losses, unexpected setbacks. Not moral failure. Not spiritual attack. Not human evil. Just life.

Paul wrote that creation itself "groans" (Romans 8:22).

We live in bodies that decay.
We face circumstances beyond our control.
Not everything is a divine test.
Not everything is an attack.
Sometimes life simply hurts.

A young man named *Jared* learned this painfully. A promising athlete, he suffered a sudden spinal injury in a car accident. He came to church asking, "Why would God break my dreams?" But over time, as he healed emotionally, he discovered a new calling—working with other young men battling discouragement. His accident was not God's punishment, but God's grace writing a new story on unexpected pages.

Brokenness often arrives through the cracks of a fallen world, but God enters those cracks with healing, comfort, and purpose.

Brokenness as the Doorway to Grace

Brokenness is painful, but it is never pointless.

In God's economy, brokenness is often the precursor to greatness.

Grace flows most freely where pride is shattered. Scripture declares: *"God opposes the proud but gives grace to the humble."* (James 4:6)

Grace is not attracted to strength—it is attracted to weakness. Grace does not flow to the self-sufficient—it flows to the surrendered.

Joseph's dungeon became the doorway to his destiny.

Paul's thorn became the revelation of God's power.

Peter's failure became the launchpad of his ministry.

David's tears became the songs that still heal hearts today.

Job's ashes became the soil of double restoration.

Brokenness strips away everything we rely on—our abilities, our pride, our illusions of control—so that we may receive what we could never earn: the grace of God.

A pastor once shared with me that his greatest season of fruitfulness came right after his most painful season of brokenness. He had lost a loved one, his ministry faced conflict, and he felt emotionally and spiritually drained. But in that place, he discovered the sustaining presence of God like never before. "I used to preach from knowledge," he said, "but after that season, I preached from compassion."

Brokenness gave him a new heart.

That's what grace does.

- ✓ *It doesn't patch us; it rebuilds us.*
- ✓ *It doesn't repair us in the shadows; it restores us in the open.*
- ✓ *It doesn't hide the scars; it fills them with gold.*

The Purpose Behind the Pain

If you are a pastor or counselor, you know this truth well: people rarely look to God when everything is perfect. Brokenness opens the soul like nothing else. It is often the only season when walls fall, egos crumble, tears flow, and honest prayers rise.

If you are an individual walking through brokenness, hear this: God is not teaching you a lesson out of anger. He is drawing you into His heart. He is removing what hinders intimacy and revealing what strengthens faith.

Brokenness is not God's rejection—it is His redirection.

It is not the end of the story—it is the doorway into a new chapter.

It is the place where we stop holding on to our strength and start depending on His.

And most of all, brokenness is the place where God writes His most beautiful stories—stories like

Joseph's, stories like David's, stories like Paul's… and stories like yours.

Job: Broken but Blessed

There is a particular kind of silence that falls when suffering enters a person's life—the silence after the doctor delivers the diagnosis, after the spouse walks away, after the business collapses, after the accident changes everything. It is the silence between breaths when the mind tries to understand what the heart refuses to accept.

Job lived in that silence.

And in that silence, he discovered God in a way he never had before.

Job's story is not simply the story of a man who suffered. It is the story of a man whose pain became the birthplace of revelation—whose brokenness became the doorway to blessing.

The Collapse of Everything Familiar

When we read Job's story, we must remember that he was not an average man. Scripture describes him as "blameless and upright," a man who feared God and shunned evil (Job 1:1). He was wealthy, respected, and deeply rooted in faith. If anyone appeared untouchable, it was Job.

Then, in a series of devastating blows, everything collapsed.

His livestock vanished, his servants were killed, his children died in a tragic accident, and his health deteriorated into unbearable agony. What took years to build was destroyed in a single day. The man who once sat with elders at the city gates now sat in ashes, scraping his wounds with broken pottery.

This is not merely the story of loss—it is the story of identity collapse.

When grief strikes, it attacks more than circumstances. It attacks the foundations of who we believe we are. A mother whose child dies no longer knows who she is. A successful man whose business crumbles feels stripped of value. A woman whose husband abandons her questions her worth.

Job went through all three kinds of loss—family, fortune, and physical health. And yet, in the middle of the ashes, he made one of the most profound declarations in Scripture: *"The Lord gave, and the Lord has taken away; blessed be the name of the Lord"* (Job 1:21).

Job's faith did not deny the pain. It declared God's goodness despite the pain.

The Psychological Weight of Grief

Psychologists tell us that grief follows a pattern—shock, denial, anger, bargaining, depression, and eventually acceptance. Job walked through each step, often unpredictably and painfully.

He experienced shock when everything fell apart so suddenly.

He experienced denial when he wished his birth had been erased.

He expressed anger, but he directed it honestly toward God rather than pretending to be strong.

He bargained, pleading for answers that never came.

He sank into despair, saying, "My days have no meaning" (Job 7:16).

Many people wrongly assume that strong believers should not feel the depths of grief. But Job teaches us something essential: deep grief is not a sign of weak faith; it is the evidence of deep love and deep loss.

I once walked with a man named *Daniel*, who lost his wife after a prolonged illness. He was a man of faith, but for months he woke up trembling, asking God, "Why did You let this happen?" His mind knew what Scripture said, but his heart felt betrayed. His tears were not rebellion—they were human. They were the honest cries of a broken soul searching for meaning.

Over time, Daniel discovered that grieving is not the opposite of trusting God. Grieving is part of trusting God—because grief brings us to the place where we finally depend on Him for comfort no one else can give.

When Friends Fail You

One of the most painful aspects of Job's suffering was not the boils on his skin or the graves of his children—it was the misjudgment of his friends.

Eliphaz, Bildad, and Zophar meant well, but they assumed Job had sinned.

To them, brokenness could only mean punishment.

Instead of comfort, they gave criticism.

Instead of presence, they gave lectures.

Many suffering people today carry the added burden of others' opinions.

I met a woman named *Sonia*, whose husband passed away unexpectedly. Instead of receiving comfort, she heard members of her extended family whisper, "Maybe God is judging her." Their words crushed her heart far more than her widowhood.

Job's story teaches us that when someone is in pain, what they need is not answers—they need compassion.

Comfort is not found in explanations; it is found in presence.

God's Silence Is Not God's Absence

One of the most difficult parts of Job's journey was that for a long time, God said nothing.

He did not explain.

He did not justify.

He did not correct the friends.

He simply allowed the process.

This silence was not abandonment.

It was preparation.

God was guiding Job into the deepest revelation of his life—not through sermons, but through suffering.

Not through answers, but through encounter.

When God finally spoke from the whirlwind, He did not explain the reasons for the suffering. Instead, He revealed His nature. He showed Job the power of His creation, the depth of His wisdom, and the tenderness of His care. And that revelation changed everything.

Job then uttered the words that echo through eternity: *"My ears had heard of You, but now my eyes have seen You."* (Job 42:5)

Brokenness moved Job from knowing about God to experiencing God.

Suffering → Revelation

Every person walking with God undergoes this shift at some point. There is the God we hear about in sermons—the God we read about in devotions— and the God we meet in the ashes.

The God of head knowledge becomes the God of heart revelation.

Before his suffering, Job knew God as a provider.

After his suffering, Job knew God as a Father.

Before his suffering, Job worshiped from blessing.

After his suffering, Job worshiped from revelation.

Before his suffering, Job trusted God's gifts.
After his suffering, Job trusted God's heart.
In the New Testament, the same pattern appears.
Mary and Martha had heard Jesus teach. But it was only when Lazarus died that they declared, *"Lord, we believe You are the Christ."* Their loss became the canvas for Jesus' greatest revelation.
Sometimes God allows brokenness because revelation requires space. And sometimes the only space large enough is the place where everything else has fallen away.

Blessed Beyond the Pain

By the end of Job's journey, God restored him—double for all he had lost.
Not because Job earned it. Not because God owed it. But because brokenness had prepared him to receive a deeper kind of blessing.
The blessing was not just the livestock or the wealth.
The blessing was not even the restored health.
The true blessing was the revelation of God Himself.
God did not bless Job because he suffered. God blessed Job because he allowed suffering to lead him closer to God rather than farther away.

Ministering to the Suffering—A Pastoral Insight

For pastors, counselors, and ministry workers, Job's story offers sacred wisdom. Suffering people do not need quick answers.
They do not need formulas.
They do not need theological debates. They need a safe space to cry, question, doubt, and grieve.
They need someone who listens without assuming.
They need someone who sits with them in the ashes, not above them in judgment.

When counseling a person like *Anand*, who battled depression after losing his job, I discovered something important: he didn't need me to tell him God had a plan. He needed me to remind him that God had a heart.

He needed presence before promises. Compassion before counsel. Understanding before instruction.

Job's story teaches us to be careful with our words in the presence of suffering.

A grieving soul needs gentle hands, patient love, and a heart that reflects the tenderness of God.

The Invitation Hidden in the Ashes

Job's life stands as a testimony to every broken heart: God does not abandon you in your suffering. God is not silent because He is absent. God is silent because He is preparing something deeper. If you find yourself in ashes today, know this: revelation is coming.

The God you have heard about will become the God you see.

The God you believed in will become the God you experience.

Brokenness will not be the end. It will be the transformation.

And you will emerge not only restored, but changed—blessed beyond what you ever imagined.

Because in God's kingdom, brokenness is not a final chapter. It is simply the page where revelation begins.

David: Brokenness Through Sin, Shame & Restoration

There are few stories in Scripture that capture the human heart quite like the story of David. His life is a paradox—warrior and worshipper, shepherd and king, poet and fighter, a man after God's own heart yet capable of some of the darkest failures recorded in Scripture. David's brokenness did not come from persecution, betrayal, or injustice like Job's. It came from something far more painful: his own choices.

There is a unique kind of brokenness that comes not from what others have done to us but from what we have done to ourselves. This is the brokenness born out of sin, regret, shame, and moral failure. And in that brokenness, David's story becomes a mirror for every believer who has ever wondered, *"Is there grace for failures like mine?"*

The Night Everything Changed

Scripture tells it plainly. On a night when kings went to war, David stayed home. He was in the wrong place at the wrong time with a heart that had slowly grown comfortable. From the palace rooftop he saw Bathsheba, and desire overtook discernment. What followed was a series of decisions that spiraled into adultery, deception, and eventually murder.

David tried to cover it. He tried to control it. But sin has a way of exposing us no matter how deep we bury it.

When the prophet Nathan confronted him with the parable of the stolen lamb and declared, "You are the man," David's heart shattered. This was not the breaking caused by enemies. This was the breaking caused by truth.

Failure had found him. Shame engulfed him. And the man who once danced before the Lord now collapsed before Him.

Psalm 51 — The Cry of a Shattered Soul

It is in this context that Psalm 51 comes alive. This is not a theological poem. This is the cry of a man drowning in his own guilt:

"Have mercy on me, O God…"

"My sin is ever before me…"

"Against You, and You only, have I sinned…"

"Create in me a clean heart…"

"Restore to me the joy of Your salvation…"

David's repentance was not shallow. It was not remorse for getting caught. It was deep, honest, trembling brokenness. The Hebrew words he uses reflect the agony of a soul turning itself inside-out before God.

He does not blame Bathsheba.

He does not blame circumstances.

He does not excuse his behavior.

He owns his sin with raw honesty.

David teaches us that the path to restoration begins with truth—not polished prayers, not excuses, not religious performance, but truth in the inward parts.

The Weight of Shame

Shame is heavier than guilt. Guilt says, "I did something wrong." Shame whispers, "I am something wrong." And shame does not remain silent; it fills the mind with questions:

- ✓ *"How could you?"*
- ✓ *"What kind of believer does this?"*

- ✓ *"God must be done with you."*
- ✓ *"People will never forget."*

David felt that weight. He felt the sting of his moral failure. He felt the broken trust of his people. He felt the silence of God in the aftermath. And he felt what many feel today: the fear that failure has disqualified him forever.

I once counseled a man named *Rakesh*, a respected church volunteer who fell into an affair. When he confessed, he trembled uncontrollably. "I've destroyed everything," he sobbed. "My marriage, my testimony, my ministry… God will never use me again."

His shame was suffocating. He could barely look me in the eye. He believed forgiveness was possible but restoration? He thought that was for better people. Holier people. People who hadn't crashed so terribly.

But Rakesh eventually discovered what David discovered: God's mercy runs deeper than human failure. The God who sees our worst also knows our best. The God who confronts our sin also restores our soul.

The Consequences and the Mercy

David faced consequences—painful ones. Sin always leaves a trail. But consequences are not the same as condemnation. Even in the aftermath of discipline, the grace of God wrapped itself around David's life. God did not strip him of his calling. God did not remove His covenant. God did not discard him as a leader. God did not withdraw His Spirit.

In fact, David's greatest writings—the psalms that comfort the brokenhearted today—were written from the soil of his own brokenness.

This is the paradox of grace:

God does not waste even our failures.
He transforms them into testimonies.

The Restoration of a King

The restoration of David was not instantaneous. God rebuilt him slowly:

- ✓ His relationship with God was restored first.
- ✓ His joy returned.
- ✓ His worship deepened.
- ✓ His leadership matured.
- ✓ His heart softened.
- ✓ And his compassion grew.

David's later years were marked by wisdom, humility, tenderness, and a depth of worship that could only have come from someone who had been shattered and rebuilt.

Lessons from the New Testament

David's story finds echoes in the New Testament in the life of Peter. His failure came not from lust but from fear. He denied Jesus three times, ran from the courtyard in tears, and believed his calling was finished. But Jesus did not discard him. He cooked breakfast for him on the shore and restored him with gentle questions:
"Do you love Me?" "Feed My sheep."
Just as God restored David, Jesus restored Peter. And Peter went on to lead thousands.
Failure did not cancel calling. Brokenness did not invalidate purpose. Shame did not outweigh grace.

God Uses Even the Morally Broken

This is one of the most powerful lessons David's story offers: God does not use perfect people; He uses honest ones.

Morally broken people who repent deeply become spiritually powerful people who walk humbly.

I once knew a woman named *Maria*, a leader in her church who struggled secretly with pornography. The shame nearly crushed her. When she finally confessed, she expected judgment. Instead, she received prayer, accountability, and support. Today, she leads a ministry that helps young women walk in purity. Her greatest wound became her greatest assignment.

God's pattern has always been the same:

- ✓ Abraham lied—yet he became the father of faith.
- ✓ Moses murdered—yet he became the deliverer of Israel.
- ✓ Rahab was a prostitute—yet she entered the genealogy of Christ.
- ✓ Peter denied Jesus—yet he became the foundation of the early church.
- ✓ Paul persecuted believers—yet he wrote half the New Testament.
- ✓ David committed adultery and murder—yet God called him "a man after My own heart."

God does not erase the broken chapters. He redeems them.

He does not hide the testimonies. He shapes them.

He does not cover the cracks. He fills them with grace.

The Heart After God's Own Heart

A heart after God's own heart is not a flawless heart. It is a repentant one.

David's greatness was not that he never sinned—it was that he always returned to God. His brokenness did not push him away from God; it pulled him towards God. His repentance was not a moment—it was a posture.

And in that posture, God restored him.

This is the invitation for every believer who has stumbled, fallen, or failed:

- ✓ *Come back.*
- ✓ *Confess honestly.*
- ✓ *Let God rebuild what sin tried to destroy.*
- ✓ *Allow grace to do what human strength cannot.*
- ✓ *Let the God who restored David restore you.*

For in God's workshop, even the morally broken are not discarded—they are transformed. And sometimes, the most powerful testimonies come not from those who never fell, but from those who fell deeply, repented sincerely, and rose again by the mercy of God.

Moses: The Power of Holy Frustration

There are many kinds of brokenness in the lives of God's people—brokenness caused by pain, brokenness caused by sin, brokenness caused by loss. But one of the most surprising and least discussed forms of brokenness is the kind that comes through holy frustration. This is the frustration that arises not from rebellion, but from responsibility; not from self-seeking, but from calling; not from wickedness, but from the weight of leadership. And no biblical character embodies this struggle more than Moses.

Moses was chosen, called, anointed, and empowered. Yet he was also frustrated, exhausted, angry, misunderstood, and often overwhelmed. And God used that very frustration as sandpaper—the holy, divine sanding away of pride, impulsiveness, self-reliance, and raw emotion—to shape him into the leader Israel needed.

Holy frustration is not evidence of God's displeasure. It is evidence of God's preparation.

A Leader Born in Chaos

Moses' life began with turmoil. He entered the world at a time when Hebrew infants were being slaughtered. His very survival was a miracle—rescued in a basket, raised in a palace, trained in Egyptian royalty, yet connected to Hebrew bondage. He lived between two worlds, never fully belonging to either.

This tension formed in him a deep sense of justice and compassion. Scripture says that when he saw an

Egyptian beating a Hebrew slave, Moses' anger erupted. Instead of pausing, thinking, or waiting for God's timing, Moses acted impulsively—killing the Egyptian and burying the body in sand.

This was the first sign of a leader whose passion outweighed his patience, whose zeal outran his wisdom, and whose sense of justice was not yet surrendered to God's sovereignty.

His frustration with injustice was holy, but his response was human.

The Desert: God's School of Sandpaper

Moses fled to Midian and spent forty years in anonymity. The man who once walked in marble halls now walked behind sheep. The man who once had servants now served a shepherd. The man who once lived in mansions now slept under stars. But in that desert, God was sanding away the rough edges—tempering anger, softening pride, reshaping identity.

No one likes God's sandpaper seasons. They feel like demotion, not development. But God never wastes a desert.

I once met a pastor named *Elijah Fernandes*, a bold, fiery preacher who led his congregation with authority and passion. But beneath his zeal was impatience—a quick temper, a harsh tone, a tendency to push instead of shepherd. When conflict arose in his church and several families left, Elijah experienced his own "Midian moment." He stepped down temporarily, burdened by shame and confusion.

During that season, he told me something profound: "I never knew how sharp my edges were until God put me in a place where nothing worked. It was like

He stripped me down so He could build me up again—gentler, slower, softer."

Moses' desert served the same purpose. God was preparing him not for a sprint, but for a lifelong marathon of leadership. The desert was where Moses learned patience. It was where he learned to listen. It was where he learned that the work of God must be done in the strength of God, not in the strength of man.

A Leader Called Into Fire

Then came the burning bush—a flame that did not consume. A divine symbol of Moses' future. *Moses, you will burn, but you will not be consumed.*

In the fire, Moses heard the call: *"I have seen their misery… I have heard their cry… and I am sending you"* (Exodus 3:7–10).

But Moses had changed. The young impulsive prince had become a hesitant shepherd.

Once overconfident, now insecure.

Once aggressive, now cautious.

Once self-reliant, now painfully aware of his imperfections.

This, too, was holy frustration—the tension between calling and inadequacy. The frustration of knowing what God wants you to do but feeling deeply incapable of doing it.

Every pastor, counselor, and leader knows that tension. Every person called to serve understands that burning bush moment when God's call feels bigger than your courage.

Anger in the Wilderness

But Moses' transformation was not complete. Even as he obeyed, his old struggle resurfaced—anger.

- ✓ *At Pharaoh.*
- ✓ *At Israel.*
- ✓ *At their complaints.*
- ✓ *At their unbelief.*
- ✓ *At their ingratitude.*

Moses was burdened not by disobedient people alone, but by the crushing responsibility of leading broken people while being broken himself.

In Exodus 32, when Israel worshipped the golden calf, Moses' anger "burned hot," and he smashed the stone tablets. His frustration was righteous, but still uncontrolled.

In Numbers 20, anger cost him everything. God asked him to speak to the rock. Instead, Moses struck it twice—shouting, "Must we bring water out for you?" His frustration turned into self-reliance, and in that moment, he took credit for God's work. God, in His holiness, told Moses he would not enter the Promised Land.

This was not punishment—it was refinement.

Not rejection—it was recalibration.

God was showing Moses that anger may feel justified, but it cannot lead God's people.

Holy frustration must always be sanctified frustration.

The Weight of Leadership Burnout

Burnout is not modern; Moses experienced it long before therapists named it.

He was surrounded by complaints, demands, and expectations. He dealt with constant conflict. He mediated disputes. He carried the emotional burden of an entire nation.

In Numbers 11, Moses reached a breaking point. He said to God:

"I cannot carry all these people alone… the burden is too heavy for me. If this is how You intend to treat me, please go ahead and kill me." (Numbers 11:14–15)

These are the words of a leader drowning in his calling.

Pastors know this feeling.

Counselors know this feeling.

Parents know this feeling.

Anyone who carries emotional weight knows this feeling.

This is why Moses' story is so important—it shows that even the greatest leaders break. And God meets them in their breaking.

God's Leadership Sandpaper

In response to Moses' collapse, God did something beautiful. He did not scold Moses. He did not shame him. He did not tell him to "be strong." Instead, God lightened his load by giving him seventy elders to share the burden.

God did not remove Moses' calling—He redistributed the weight.

This is how God shapes leaders:

- ✓ *He breaks the illusion that ministry is carried by a single person.*
- ✓ *He dismantles pride disguised as responsibility.*
- ✓ *He replaces isolation with community.*

I once walked with a ministry leader named *Pastor Nathan*, who nearly burned out after years of carrying every role—preaching, counseling, administration, worship, youth ministry. His exhaustion turned into frustration with his congregation. *"They expect too much,"* he told me. *"I'm only human."*

God eventually led him to raise and train leaders around him. The moment he shared ministry, the tone of his voice changed. His sermons softened. His anger dissolved. His compassion returned.
Like Moses, God sanded away his need to carry everything.

The Moses Who Emerges

By the end of his life, Moses was not the hot-headed prince, nor the impulsive avenger, nor the frustrated leader. He became a man marked by humility. Scripture says:
"Now Moses was more humble than any man on earth." (Numbers 12:3)
This humility wasn't natural—it was formed.
Forged. Refined in fire. Hammered by responsibility. Softened by compassion. And shaped by holy frustration. Moses became the leader he was because God allowed the frustrating moments that reshaped him from the inside out.

Lessons for Leaders, Pastors, and Ministry Workers

Moses teaches every leader a sacred truth:

- ✓ *Frustration is not a sign that you are failing—it is a sign that God is forming you.*
- ✓ *When you feel people are too difficult, it means God is shaping your patience.*
- ✓ *When you feel the burden is too heavy, God is teaching you to delegate.*
- ✓ *When anger rises, God is revealing hidden parts that need healing.*
- ✓ *When burnout creeps in, God is inviting you to rest, to trust, to share the load.*

- ✓ *When your strength feels insufficient, God is preparing to show His strength in you.*

Holy frustration is one of God's greatest tools.
It is painful, yes. But it is purposeful.
It exposes what must change.
It refines what must grow.
It reveals what must die so that what is divine may live.

The Grace Behind the Frustration

What makes Moses' story so comforting is this:
God never gave up on him.
Not in Egypt. Not in Midian. Not in the wilderness. Not at the rock.
God walked with him, shaped him, corrected him, restored him, and loved him.
In the New Testament, Moses appears again standing beside Jesus on the Mount of Transfiguration. The man who couldn't enter the earthly Promised Land was granted entrance into the heavenly one.
That is the grace of God toward leaders who break.
God does not discard frustrated leaders. He transforms them into shepherds after His heart.
And the Moses who emerges from holy frustration becomes the Moses who can carry the weight of a nation—not because he is strong, but because his rough edges have been smoothed by the gentle hands of a patient God.

Paul: From Wounder to Healer

There is a kind of brokenness that feels almost impossible to redeem—the brokenness of being wrong. Terribly wrong. Hurtfully wrong. The brokenness of realizing that your words, actions, and convictions have wounded others, misled others, and even destroyed others. This kind of brokenness is not caused by tragedy or betrayal… but by truth. The truth that you were the one causing harm. The truth that you were the one breaking others.

No biblical character embodies this transformation better than Saul of Tarsus—the man the world would later know as Paul. His story is not simply a tale of conversion; it is the journey of a wounder becoming a healer. Of a man blinded by pride becoming a man enlightened by grace. Of a persecutor becoming a pastor. Of a destroyer becoming a builder. His entire ministry was birthed out of a brokenness so deep, so humbling, and so shattering, that it turned the world upside down.

Paul teaches us that God does not merely save broken people—He reshapes them into instruments of healing for others.

The Arrogance That Led to Blindness

Before he became an apostle, Saul was a man consumed by certainty. He believed he understood God perfectly. He believed his zeal made him righteous. He believed his education, lineage, and discipline made him superior. In Philippians 3, Paul describes his former self with a painful honesty:

"Hebrew of Hebrews."

"Pharisee."

"As for zeal, persecuting the church."
"As for righteousness based on the law, faultless."
His identity was built on performance, perfection, and pride.
This prideful certainty made Saul dangerous. He wasn't a passive unbeliever—he was aggressive, confident, passionate, and relentless. He hunted Christians, dragged families from their homes, approved of Stephen's execution, and was feared across Judea.
Paul did not become broken because of hardship. He became broken because God confronted his pride. It was this pride that brought him face to face with divine light on the Damascus road. And with one heavenly flash, the man who believed he could see better than everyone became blind.
Pride leads to blindness.
Blindness leads to surrender.
Surrender leads to transformation.

The Moment His World Collapsed
Acts 9 records the moment Saul encountered Jesus. A light brighter than the sun, a voice that shook the ground, and a question that pierced his soul:
"Saul, Saul, why are you persecuting Me?"
Not "My church."
Not "My people."
Not "My disciples."
But Me.
In that moment, Saul realized that he had been attacking the very One he thought he was serving.
This was the shattering moment. Not the light. Not the blindness. But the truth.
He was wrong. Violently wrong. Sinfully wrong. Dangerously wrong.

God broke him not with punishment but with revelation. The revelation that grace had come for him—not because he deserved it, but because Jesus loved him.

Brokenness That Leads to Silence

For three days, Saul was blind. He ate nothing. Drank nothing. Spoke nothing. It was as if God placed him inside a divine cocoon—a place where everything went quiet so that everything inside could change.

Every counselor knows that transformation often begins in silence.

Every coach knows that clarity often comes after collapse.

Every believer knows that God sometimes removes all distractions just to speak one truth: "*You are not who you think you are. But you can become who I know you are.*"

During those three days, Saul's identity was stripped. His confidence dissolved. His pride shattered. His theology turned upside down. He was forced to confront the darkest truth of his life: he was the wounder, not the healer.

This was holy brokenness.

Ananias: The Counselor God Sent

When God spoke to Ananias, the man hesitated. "Lord, I have heard many reports about this man..." (Acts 9:13). Even God's people were afraid of Saul. But God insisted:

"He is My chosen instrument."

This is a counselor's verse. This is a coach's mandate. This is hope for every family dealing with someone difficult, destructive, or damaged.

The people who have caused the most hurt may one day bring the most healing.

Ananias laid hands on Saul—touching the man everyone feared—and said the most shocking word:

"Brother."

Brother?

How could he call him brother?

How could trust form so quickly?

How could grace flow so freely?

But isn't that how Christ receives us?

The scales fell off Saul's eyes, and with them fell his pride, his prejudice, and his false righteousness. He rose from that house a new man—with a new name, a new identity, and a new mission.

Paul's Brokenness Became His Message

Paul never forgot who he used to be. He referred to himself as:

"The chief of sinners." (1 Timothy 1:15)

"Unworthy to be an apostle." (1 Corinthians 15:9)

"One shown mercy." (1 Timothy 1:16)

His brokenness was not a scar he hid. It was the testimony he preached.

He spoke often of his past—not to glorify sin, but to magnify grace.

In the Old Testament, Jacob limped after wrestling with God. That limp became his reminder of grace. In the New Testament, Paul carried a different kind of limp—memory. The memory of the people he hurt, the prayers he silenced, the fear he caused. And yet, God used that very limp to shape his ministry.

Brokenness was not a burden in Paul's life; it was fuel.

When a Wounder Becomes a Healer

Paul's ministry changed the world because he understood broken hearts.
He felt deep compassion for new believers.
He wept for churches under attack.
He carried spiritual children in his prayers.
He strengthened the weak, comforted the sorrowful, and confronted with gentleness.

I once knew a man named *John Mathew*, a former gang leader in his youth. He was feared, reckless, violent, and destructive. But after a radical encounter with Christ in his early twenties, he slowly transformed. Years later, John became one of the most empathetic counselors I ever met. He led a ministry for young men struggling with anger, addiction, and rage.
He told me something I'll never forget: *"I know what It feels like to break someone. That's why God now uses me to build them."*
Paul would have said the same.
The people who once wounded deeply often become the ones who heal compassionately.

The Global Impact of a Broken Servant

Paul's influence did not come from talent alone. It came from tenderness.
Not from intellect alone. But from empathy.
Not from strength alone. But from weakness.
This is why he wrote:
"His power is made perfect in weakness." (2 Corinthians 12:9)
Paul understood that the broken places in his soul became channels of God's power. His thorn kept him

humble. His past kept him compassionate. His suffering kept him close to God.
From prison cells to shipwrecks, from rejection to betrayal, from beatings to loneliness, Paul's ministry was shaped not by comfort but by brokenness. And yet, this broken vessel carried the gospel farther than any other apostle.

New Testament Reflection: Peter and Paul
Peter denied Jesus; Paul persecuted Him.
Peter failed out of fear; Paul failed out of pride.
Peter was restored on a shoreline; Paul was restored on a roadside.
Both men became pillars of the early church.
God did not choose flawless men. He chose broken ones. Because only the broken truly understand the need for grace.

Application for Counselors, Coaches, and Ministry Leaders
Paul teaches us that the most effective counselors are not the ones who have it all together, but the ones who have walked through darkness and emerged with compassion.
Counselors who once felt unforgiven help others believe God forgives.
Coaches who once felt unworthy help others find identity.
Pastors who once carried pride now shepherd with humility.
Parents who once wounded their children now heal with tenderness.
People trust healers who carry their own scars.
Your past does not disqualify you. Your failures do not silence you. Your brokenness does not weaken

you. Like Paul, your greatest ministry may be born from the very place where God broke you.

From Broken to Built

Paul's life reminds us that God does not choose as the world chooses.

He does not scan the earth for perfect vessels. He looks for surrendered ones.

Saul was shattered by truth. Healed by grace. And rebuilt by purpose.

A wounder became a healer. A persecutor became a preacher. A self-righteous Pharisee became a servant of Christ.

This is the masterpiece of God's restoration:

- ✓ *He takes the most unlikely person and gives him the greatest assignment.*
- ✓ *He takes the most broken vessel and makes it carry the richest treasure.*
- ✓ *He takes the most painful past and turns it into the most powerful ministry.*

And He can do the same with you.

Peter: Broken by Failure, Restored by Love

There are failures... and then there are failures that shake you to the core. Failures that make you question your worth, your identity, your sincerity, your faith, and even your future with God. The kind of failures that echo inside the heart long after the moment has passed. This was the kind of failure Peter experienced on the night he denied Jesus.

Peter was not just any disciple. He was part of Jesus' inner circle—the man who walked on water, the first to declare Jesus as the Christ, the one who vowed he would never leave or betray his Master. Peter wasn't weak. He wasn't faithless. He wasn't insincere. He simply broke under pressure.

And because of that, his story has become healing for anyone who has failed repeatedly, anyone who has made promises they couldn't keep, anyone who has loved Jesus deeply yet stumbled grievously, and anyone who feels unworthy of God's call.

The Confidence Before the Collapse

Peter was bold, emotional, affectionate, loud, sincere, passionate, loyal, and impulsive. That combination made him powerful on the mountaintop and vulnerable in the valley.

The night before Jesus was arrested, Jesus told His disciples that they would all fall away. Peter, with all the sincerity of his heart, insisted:

"Even if everyone else deserts You, I will not." (Mark 14:29)

He wasn't lying.

He meant every word.

He loved Jesus fiercely.
But sincerity is not the same as strength.
This is the illusion many believers live with. We believe our intentions are enough to carry us. But intentions alone cannot sustain us through temptation, fear, or spiritual warfare.
Peter loved Jesus—but fear loved Peter too.

The Night Fear Crushed Him
When Judas arrived with the soldiers, Peter tried to fight—he drew his sword and struck the servant's ear. But when Jesus told him to put away the sword, Peter's confidence crumbled. He didn't know how to follow Jesus into weakness.
As Jesus was taken away, Peter followed from a distance. Distance is dangerous. Distance from Jesus often leads to denial. At the courtyard, fear gripped him. The cold night air carried whispers. The light of a charcoal fire flickered on his face. A servant girl recognized him—he denied it. Another girl pointed him out—he denied it again.
A man declared, "Surely you are one of them"—and Peter cursed and denied Jesus a third time.
Then a rooster crowed.
Luke records a heartbreaking detail: *"The Lord turned and looked straight at Peter."* (Luke 22:61)
One look from Jesus—and Peter fell apart inside.
He didn't see anger.
He didn't see disappointment.
He didn't see condemnation.
He saw love. Sorrow. Understanding. Compassion.
The look that broke him… was love.
And Peter ran out into the night, weeping bitterly—a grown man sobbing not from fear but from shame.

The Heavy Weight of Repeated Failure

Shame is not loud. It whispers. It tells you:

"You're a hypocrite."

"You're too weak."

"You don't deserve forgiveness."

"You can't be trusted."

"God is done with you."

Peter carried this shame through the darkest night of his life.

Even after Jesus rose again, Peter felt unworthy.

Even after seeing the empty tomb, Peter stayed silent.

Even after meeting Jesus in the upper room, Peter stayed distant.

He believed in resurrection—he just didn't believe in restoration.

Many believers feel that way today. They come to church but feel unworthy. They worship but feel disqualified. They read Scripture but feel distant.

I once counseled a woman named *Rachel*, a gentle mother of two who had struggled with alcohol secretly for years. She loved Jesus, served faithfully, and truly desired to change. But each time she relapsed, the shame grew heavier.

"I feel like Peter," she told me, tears filling her eyes. *"I love Him so much. But I keep failing. How many times will He forgive me?"*

The story of Peter exists precisely for people like Rachel—for those who think they've gone too far, failed too many times, or disappointed God too deeply.

The God Who Makes Breakfast for Failures

The most beautiful part of Peter's story takes place by a quiet shoreline in John 21. Peter had gone back to fishing—not because he lost faith, but because he lost faith in himself.

He felt the calling was too great for a failure like him.

At dawn, Jesus stood on the shore and called out to them. When Peter recognized Him, he didn't wait for the boat to reach land. He jumped into the water and swam.

Failure didn't stop him from pursuing Jesus. Shame slows us down, but love still pulls us forward.

On the shore, Jesus had already prepared a charcoal fire—the same kind of fire where Peter denied Him. Jesus was recreating the scene not to condemn Peter, but to heal him.

Three denials.

Three questions. *"Do you love Me?"*

Jesus was not testing Peter—He was restoring him. He was rebuilding Peter's heart, brick by brick, word by word. Peter had denied knowing Jesus. Now Jesus invited him to declare his love. *"Feed My sheep,"* Jesus said.

Not *"prove yourself."*

Not *"earn it back."*

Not *"restart from zero."*

He restored Peter instantly and completely.

The Old Testament Echo: Jonah

Just as Peter ran from his calling because of shame, Jonah ran from his calling because of fear and prejudice. Both encountered grace in their darkest moments.

Jonah in the belly of a fish.

Peter in the courtyard of denial.

Both were given a second chance.
God's mercy is not limited. It reaches into fish bellies, courtyards, addictions, regrets, and failures. The Old Testament echoes the New: God restores those who run.

The Restoration Was Not Only Personal — It Was Missional

What's astounding about Peter's restoration is that Jesus didn't just forgive him; He re-commissioned him.
"Feed My lambs."
"Take care of My sheep."
"Feed My sheep."
Peter wasn't merely forgiven—he was entrusted.
It's as if Jesus was saying: *Your failure didn't cancel your future. Your weakness qualifies you for compassion. Your brokenness equips you to feed broken people.*
And indeed, on the Day of Pentecost, the man who denied Jesus became the man who declared Him boldly to thousands. Peter's failure became the soil where his calling grew.

Application for Families, Parents & Backsliders

Peter's story is hope for:

- ✓ *Parents who worry they've failed their children.*
- ✓ *Spouses who regret words they can't take back.*
- ✓ *Children who drift away and wonder if God still wants them.*
- ✓ *Backsliders who think they've crossed the point of return.*
- ✓ *Families torn by repeated mistakes.*

One evening, a father named *Samuel* confessed to me with trembling hands, *"I've yelled too much. I've hurt my children with my words. I love them, but I don't know how to fix this."*
I reminded him of Peter.
If Jesus restored a man who denied Him during His darkest hour, He can restore a father who lost his temper, a mother who feels overwhelmed, a youth who has drifted away, a spouse who regrets their decisions.
Restoration is not God's *secondary* plan—it is His *specialty*.

Where Failure Meets Love

Peter teaches us that:

- ✓ *Love heals what shame destroys.*
- ✓ *Grace lifts what guilt crushes.*
- ✓ *Jesus restores what weakness breaks.*

Peter was not restored by a sermon.
Not by a miracle.
Not by a command.
Not by self-discipline.
He was restored by love.
A love that did not deny his failure, but healed it. A love that did not erase the memory, but redeemed it. A love that did not minimize the pain, but transformed it.
And that is how Peter, the broken fisherman, became Peter, the fearless apostle.

- ✓ *Your failure is not final.*
- ✓ *Your shame is not permanent.*
- ✓ *Your calling is not cancelled.*
- ✓ *Your story is not over.*

Because the same Jesus who made breakfast for Peter is still standing on the shores of your life—waiting to restore you with love.

Hannah: The Broken Heart That Birthed Revival

Some forms of brokenness are loud—like Peter's denial or David's moral collapse. But some are silent, hidden, and invisible to the outside world. It is the kind of brokenness buried deep within the chambers of the heart... a longing unfulfilled, a prayer unanswered, a wound carried quietly with dignity.

Hannah's story is this kind of brokenness.

She was not broken because she sinned or failed. She was broken because she had a desire so sacred, so tender, and so deeply intertwined with her identity as a woman, that its absence felt like a wound that would not close.

Hannah's brokenness did not make her bitter toward God—it made her desperate *for* God. And from the womb of her pain came a child who changed a nation.

Sometimes revival begins with a broken heart crying in a quiet corner.

The Weight Hannah Carried

Hannah was married to Elkanah, a man who deeply loved her. But in a culture where barrenness carried shame, where motherhood defined significance, Hannah felt the ache of emptiness every single day. It wasn't simply the absence of a child—it was the presence of disappointment.

Her rival, Peninnah, taunted her, reminding her of what she lacked. Scripture says that Peninnah provoked her "year after year" (1 Samuel 1:7). Every festival, every family gathering, every moment of worship became a reminder of her longing.

Brokenness often intensifies in seasons of celebration.

- ✓ *Weddings highlight singleness.*
- ✓ *Baby showers heighten infertility.*
- ✓ *Festivals magnify loneliness.*
- ✓ *Family gatherings expose family wounds.*

Hannah wept hard—but silently. Her tears were not tantrums. They were prayers.

Elkanah, like many husbands today who don't understand inner pain, tried to comfort her with words that did not reach her wound:

"Am I not better to you than ten sons?"

Good husbands mean well, but not even love can fill certain voids. Hannah's ache was a God-sized ache.

When Prayer Becomes Pain and Pain Becomes Prayer

One day, Hannah entered the tabernacle. She was not there to impress anyone. She was not there to perform a ritual. She was there to pour out her soul. Scripture says she was "in bitterness of soul" and prayed with such intensity that her lips moved but no sound came out.

Eli the priest thought she was drunk.

This is what deep brokenness looks like—people misread it, misunderstand it, and mislabel it.

Eli's accusation did not anger her. It humbled her even more. She explained, *"I am a woman of a sorrowful spirit… I have been pouring out my soul before the Lord."*

Hannah wasn't praying for a son alone—she was pouring her brokenness at God's altar. And God met her there.

Not with a miracle.

Not with a sign.

Not with a dramatic encounter.
But with a simple word: *"Go in peace, and the God of Israel grant your petition."*
(Eli didn't even know what she prayed for!)
Hannah walked away with no physical change, but with a supernatural peace. Sometimes God fixes the heart before He fixes the situation.

The New Testament Echo: Elizabeth
Hannah's story finds a beautiful parallel in the New Testament through Elizabeth, the mother of John the Baptist. She too was barren, ridiculed, and heartbroken. Scripture says she lived with the "*reproach among people*" (Luke 1:25).
Both women carried the same wound:

- ✓ *A heart longing for something deeply sacred.*
- ✓ *A desire that stretched their faith.*
- ✓ *A brokenness that pushed them into prayer instead of bitterness.*

And both bore sons who ushered in revival for their generation.
Hannah birthed Samuel—the prophet who anointed kings.
Elizabeth birthed John—the prophet who prepared the way for Christ.
Broken wombs birthed destiny.
Empty hearts became vessels of revival.

The Birth of Samuel — A Miracle Wrapped in Surrender
When God finally opened Hannah's womb, she did not cling selfishly to the child. She kept her vow. After weaning Samuel, she brought him to the tabernacle and surrendered him entirely to the service of God.
This is the most astonishing part of Hannah's story.

- ✓ *Her brokenness did not make her clingy.*
- ✓ *Her blessing did not make her arrogant.*
- ✓ *Her miracle did not make her possessive.*

Hannah handed over the very thing she prayed for.

And because she surrendered the son of her tears, God entrusted her with more. Scripture says He blessed her with many children afterward.

Brokenness purified her desire. Surrender multiplied her blessing.

Her Pain Became a Prophetic Song

After surrendering Samuel, Hannah didn't weep—she worshipped. Her prayer in 1 Samuel 2 is one of the most powerful prophetic songs in Scripture. She declared:

"My horn is exalted in the Lord."

"He raises the poor from the dust."

"He lifts the needy from the ash heap."

This is not the voice of a barren woman. This is the voice of a revived woman.

Hannah's heart healed not when she conceived Samuel, but when she surrendered Samuel.

Joy isn't found in what God gives— joy is found in trusting the One who gives.

Hannah's Story for Today's Families and Individuals

Hannah's journey mirrors the silent suffering many face today.

I once met a young wife named *Priya*, who longed desperately for a child. She avoided baby showers. She cried silently at night. Well-meaning relatives asked insensitive questions. Social media became a battlefield of emotions. She felt forgotten by God.

One day in a prayer meeting, she whispered, “I’m not angry with God… I’m just tired.” That confession opened a door of healing. Her brokenness, like Hannah’s, pushed her into deeper intimacy with God. A year later, she conceived. But more importantly, her heart found joy long before the pregnancy test ever turned positive.

I have also counseled parents who pray for their prodigal children. Spouses waiting for a marriage to heal. Families longing for reconciliation. Youth longing for purpose. Singles longing for companionship.

There is a Hannah in every church, every family, every heart.

Her story teaches us that the waiting room is not a punishment— it is where God forms revival.

The Leadership Lesson: Revival Begins with Brokenness

Samuel grew up to be a prophet who revived a spiritually dead nation. He anointed Saul and David. He restored prophetic order. He ushered Israel out of corruption and into a new era.

And it all began… with a woman on her knees, her shoulders shaking in silent agony, her lips moving in prayer, her heart breaking in surrender.

- ✓ *Revival didn’t start in the palace.*
- ✓ *Revival didn’t start in the pulpit.*
- ✓ *Revival didn’t start on a battlefield.*
- ✓ *Revival started with Hannah’s tears.*

This is the paradox of God: He births greatness from weakness. He uses sorrow to write destiny. He brings nations alive through broken hearts.

New Testament Reflection: Mary

Just as Hannah surrendered Samuel, Mary surrendered Jesus. "Hannah gave her son to the Lord." "Mary gave her son to the world."

Both were women of surrender.

Both birthed revival.

Both carried promises bigger than their pain.

God partners with surrendered people to do supernatural things.

Hannah's Brokenness Was the Womb of Israel's Restoration

- ✓ *Hannah thought she was asking for a child. God was giving her a prophet.*
- ✓ *Hannah thought she was battling barrenness. God was preparing revival.*
- ✓ *Hannah cried for personal breakthrough. God used her to break a national drought.*
- ✓ *Her brokenness birthed more than a son… it birthed a movement.*

This is the miracle of surrender: God takes the tears we give Him and turns them into testimonies that live for generations. Your brokenness may feel personal… but its impact may be eternal.

The Anatomy of a Broken Heart

Every human being carries wounds. Some are visible—etched into the body like scars from old battles. But the deepest wounds are hidden, lodged in the unseen places of the heart. They bleed quietly. They ache silently. They shape who we become and how we see the world.

Brokenness is not a single event. It is a layered experience—emotional, mental, spiritual, and relational—and each layer affects the others. When a heart breaks, it shatters in many directions. And unless we understand the anatomy of that brokenness, healing often remains incomplete.

This chapter is a gentle walk through the inner landscapes of the human heart. A journey into what hurts, why it hurts, and how God walks with us through every wound until restoration becomes possible.

1. Emotional Wounds — The Cries Behind the Silence

Emotional wounds are the injuries of the soul—pain caused by betrayal, abandonment, rejection, loss, or disappointment. These wounds often form in childhood but surface throughout life.

David expressed such wounds in the Psalms with raw honesty: *"I am poured out like water… My heart has turned to wax; it has melted within me."* —Psalm 22:14

David wasn't describing physical pain. This was emotional devastation—heart-melting grief.

Emotional wounds distort our sense of identity. They create inner messages like:

"I'm not enough."
"No one really loves me."
"I always ruin things."
"I'm destined to be alone."

I once counseled a young woman named *Meera* who carried a deep fear of abandonment. She had been raised by a single mother who worked late into the night. Though her mother loved her, the little girl inside Meera interpreted those absences as rejection. So every time a friendship felt distant or a relationship struggled, Meera fell apart internally. Her emotional wound whispered old lies: *"They will leave you too."*

It took time, prayer, and gentle conversations for her to understand that the fear wasn't coming from her present but from her past.

Emotional wounds are healed when they are named, expressed, and brought into God's light. David found healing not by pretending everything was fine—but by pouring out his heart before God.

2. Mental Wounds — The Thoughts That Chain Us

Mental wounds often accompany emotional pain. They manifest as anxious thoughts, spiraling worries, obsessive fears, and negative mental patterns that replay endlessly.

These are the wounds Paul addressed when he wrote:

"Be transformed by the renewing of your mind." — Romans 12:2

Mental wounds aren't about intelligence; they are about interpretation.

They affect how we see God, ourselves, and the world.

Some people reinterpret every disappointment as proof that God has forgotten them. Others replay failures until they believe they are failures. Some fear the future so intensely that they cannot enjoy the present.

A man named *Vikram* came to me after losing his job. He was a talented engineer, but his mind had become a battlefield. He would lie awake replaying every mistake at work. "I'm useless," he whispered one day, "God doesn't want me."

His mental wound twisted one event into a false identity.

Healing mental wounds requires truth—slow, gentle, repeated truth. Scripture is the most powerful tool here, because it doesn't just comfort emotions—it rewrites thinking: *"You are precious in My sight."* (Isaiah 43:4)

"I will never leave you." (Hebrews 13:5)

"You are fearfully and wonderfully made." (Psalm 139:14)

God's Word doesn't erase wounds instantly, but it builds new pathways inside the mind— pathways that lead to peace instead of fear.

3. Spiritual Wounds — When God Feels Silent

Spiritual wounds are the most misunderstood wounds of all. They occur when a believer experiences unanswered prayers, spiritual dryness, church hurt, or disappointment in God.

Job expressed this kind of wound when he cried: *"Where are You?"* —Job 23:3

Job didn't lose faith—he lost spiritual clarity. His world collapsed so suddenly that he couldn't understand why God allowed it. His questions were not rebellious; they were relational.

Spiritual wounds often develop in silence—when a believer continues to pray but feels unseen, continues to worship but feels empty, continues to serve but feels alone.

A young mother named *Anita* once told me, "I feel guilty even saying this... but I feel like God is ignoring me." She had prayed earnestly for her marriage to survive. Instead, it ended painfully. Her heart broke—and her faith felt bruised.

In Scripture, even Jesus expressed spiritual agony: "My God, My God, why have You forsaken Me?" (Matthew 27:46).

This means we are safe to bring our spiritual confusion to God.

We can bring tears. Questions. Doubts. Silence.

God heals spiritual wounds through His presence—not always immediately, but faithfully. Like He did for Elijah, who lay under a broom tree exhausted and discouraged, God often heals by whispering, *"I am still here."*

Healing spiritual wounds is less about answers and more about restored intimacy.

4. Relational Wounds — The Scars People Leave

Some of the deepest wounds come from relationships—marriages that crumble, friendships that betray, parents who wound in ignorance, children who grow distant, or churches that misunderstand.

Joseph carried such wounds. His own brothers betrayed him, sold him, lied about him, and erased him from their family. Years later, when he finally revealed himself, he wept so loudly the entire palace heard him.

Relational wounds change how we trust. They build walls we call "boundaries," but sometimes those walls become prisons.

A man named *Samuel*, a successful businessman, once shared, *"I don't let people get too close. People always disappoint. It's safer to keep connections small."* His childhood held the root—a father who broke every promise he ever made.

Relational wounds are healed in community.

Through safe people.

Through honest conversations.

Through forgiveness—not the quick, forced forgiveness that emotionally bypasses pain, but the gradual, liberating forgiveness that God works inside us.

Even Jesus experienced relational wounds—Judas betrayed Him, Peter denied Him, Thomas doubted Him. Yet He restored and embraced them.

Relational healing doesn't erase wounds—but it transforms them.

How God Heals the Layers — A Simple, Gentle Framework

While this book avoids clinical jargon, it includes insights used by counselors, pastors, and coaches—bridging Scripture with humanity.

Here is a simple model you can imagine like a four-room house:

- ✓ Room 1 — Acknowledge the Pain (Emotional Layer)

  God cannot heal what we refuse to feel. Like David, we acknowledge our sorrow, anger, loneliness, and grief—honestly.
- ✓ Room 2 — Recognize the Lies (Mental Layer)

Just as Paul taught, we identify unhealthy thoughts and replace them with truth.

- ✓ Room 3 — Return to God (Spiritual Layer)
  Like Hannah, Elijah, and Job, we bring our raw honesty to God until intimacy is restored.
- ✓ Room 4 — Repair with Others (Relational Layer)
  Forgiveness, boundaries, reconciliation, and trustworthy people process the relational wounds.

Healing moves through these rooms—not always in order, but gently, guided by the Holy Spirit.

Biblical Portrait: God Heals Broken Hearts Holistically

Psalm 147:3 says: *"He heals the brokenhearted and binds up their wounds."*

The Hebrew word for "wounds" here refers to *multiple kinds of injuries*—not just physical, but emotional, mental, spiritual, and relational.

God doesn't heal partially. He heals deeply. Completely. Tenderly. The Holy Spirit is not only a Comforter—He is a Counselor. The Father is not only a Creator—He is a Healer. Jesus is not only a Savior—He is a Restorer. Your brokenness is not random. Your pain is not wasted. Your wounds are not invisible to God. He knows every layer of your heart, and He walks through each one until you are whole again.

God the Master Craftsman: How He Rebuilds Us

There is a reason God so often compares Himself to a builder, an architect, a potter, a refiner, and a craftsman. These are not accidental metaphors. They reveal His nature—patient, precise, intentional, and unhurried. God is not a mechanic who simply replaces parts. He is an artist who restores beauty. He does not discard what is flawed; He reshapes it. He does not throw away what is cracked; He fills it with glory.

In Japan, Kintsugi artists take broken pottery and restore it not by hiding the cracks but by filling them with gold. The result is not a piece that looks repaired—it is a piece more beautiful than before the breaking. The flaws become the feature, the cracks become the crowning glory, and the scars become the story.

This is the heart of God toward the broken.

He does not hide our wounds. He heals them with glory.

He fills the fractured places with grace. And the healed scars become testimonies.

The Potter and the Clay — God's Gentle Process of Reconstruction

Jeremiah 18 paints one of the most tender pictures of God: *"Then I went down to the potter's house, and behold, he was working at the wheel… The vessel he was making was marred in his hands; so the potter made it again into another vessel, as seemed best to him."*

God did not discard the flawed clay. He did not throw it aside. He reshaped it. Brokenness does not disqualify the clay, it simply calls the potter's hands closer. Jeremiah was instructed to *watch*—to observe not the clay, but the potter. The clay did not repair itself. The clay did not complain. The clay did not direct the process. It simply yielded. This is the first and hardest step in restoration: surrender.

David understood this when he wrote in Psalm 51:17: *"A broken and contrite heart, O God, You will not despise."*

God is not attracted to our strength. He is attracted to our surrender.

Surrender Before Restoration — The Heart God Can Shape

Every rebuilding begins with a letting go— letting go of control, letting go of self-reliance, letting go of old coping mechanisms, letting go of pride, shame, and fear. God cannot rebuild what we cling to.

I remember a man named *Rohan*, who came for counseling after his marriage fell apart. He was angry, defensive, and determined to prove that he had done nothing wrong. As long as he argued, healing could not begin. One evening, he broke down completely and said, *"I don't know how to fix myself anymore."*

That was the moment restoration began. Because surrender is not failure—it is foundation. God never rushes surrender. He waits patiently until the heart softens, just like the potter waits for the clay to yield under his fingers.

Brokenness awakens surrender. Surrender invites the touch of the Master Craftsman. And once God begins to rebuild, He does so with a precision and gentleness beyond human capability.

God's Divine "Repair Stages" — The Slow, Beautiful Work of the Master Craftsman

Though God rebuilds us uniquely, Scripture reveals patterns in His craftsmanship—movements of the Spirit found in the stories of Moses, David, Job, Peter, Hannah, Joseph, and countless others. These patterns are not bullet-point steps; they are seasons—holy, sacred seasons through which God shapes us.

1. The Exposure Stage — Shining Light on the Cracks

This is when God reveals what is broken, often through circumstances, confrontation, loss, or truth that hits the soul. Peter's denial exposed his fear. David's sin was exposed through Nathan. The Prodigal's emptiness was exposed in the pigpen. Adam hid, but God called out, "Where are you?"

Exposure is painful, but it is mercy in disguise. God reveals only what He intends to heal.

A young woman named *Elina* once told me, *"Pastor, I thought God was punishing me when everything fell apart. Now I see He was showing me what I refused to face."*

God exposes not to shame, but to begin healing.

2. The Softening Stage — Preparing the Heart Like Clay

Before the potter shapes the vessel, he softens the clay. Before God shapes the soul, He often softens the heart through humility, repentance, worship, tears, or silence.

This is the season when pride falls away. When self-will surrenders. When masks are removed. When our heart finally whispers, “Lord, have Your way.”

Moses became soft in Midian. Jacob became soft after wrestling God. Paul became soft in three days of blindness. Without softening, shaping is impossible.

3. The Shaping Stage — God Reshapes Identity, Thinking, and Desire

Once the heart yields, God begins His holy craftsmanship. He reshapes how we think, how we love, how we respond, how we see ourselves, how we relate to Him. Every broken story in Scripture—Joseph, Ruth, Rahab, Esther— reveals God rebuilding identity first.

Joseph went from slave to ruler— but his heart changed long before his position did.

Rahab went from prostitute to redeemer— not because her past disappeared, but because God redefined her future.

Real transformation is not about managing behavior; it is about receiving a new identity from God.

4. The Filling Stage — God Pours His Spirit Into Broken Places

Just as Kintsugi fills cracks with gold, God fills our broken places with His Spirit. The Spirit fills fear with courage, shame with honor, emptiness with purpose, wounds with compassion.

Peter’s denial became the very place where God filled him with boldness.

Paul’s blindness became the place where God filled him with revelation.

Hannah’s tears became the place where God filled her with joy.

In God's kingdom, cracks are not flaws—they are openings.

5. The Strengthening Stage — God Builds Stability Where Weakness Was

The potter does not send a vessel into use until it is strengthened in the fire. Likewise, God strengthens us through:

- ✓ *Perseverance*
- ✓ *Discipline*
- ✓ *Consistent obedience*
- ✓ *Community*
- ✓ *Scripture*
- ✓ *Prayer*

But He does not leave us in the fire longer than needed. As He told Isaiah, *"When you walk through fire, you shall not be burned."* —Isaiah 43:2

Strengthening is never punishment. It is preparation.

6. The Commissioning Stage — God Uses the Restored to Restore Others

Once Joseph was restored, he saved nations.

Once Peter was restored, he restored others.

Once Paul was restored, he planted churches.

Once Hannah was restored, she mothered a prophet.

Once Job was restored, he became a living testimony of God's faithfulness.

God never rebuilds us just for ourselves. He rebuilds us for others.

Your story is not merely your story.

Your healing becomes someone else's hope.

Just as Kintsugi turns cracks into golden lines of beauty, God turns your scars into paths of healing for someone else's heart.

When God Rebuilds, the Result Is Greater Than the Original

Hannah's barren heart became the birthplace of Samuel. Ruth's widowhood became the doorway to the Messiah's lineage. Joseph's betrayal became the pathway to national deliverance. Peter's denial became the foundation for Pentecost. Paul's wounds became letters that changed the world.

God does not restore you to where you were— He rebuilds you into something greater, deeper, stronger, more compassionate, more Christlike, and more fruitful. Your brokenness is not the end— ***it is the beginning of a masterpiece***.

Just like the three burnt guitars I rescued— what the world throws away, the Master Craftsman rebuilds into something valuable.

Just like the old refrigerator I insisted on repairing— what others give up on, God revitalizes with a single touch.

Just like the lives in the slum church— stories written off by society, rewritten by God's redeeming grace.

Healing is not an event. It is the touch of the Master Craftsman. A touch so gentle, so patient, so divine, that the vessel which emerges carries the shine of heaven itself.

The Stages of Healing: From Hurt to Wholeness

Healing is not a straight line. It is not a moment, nor a single prayer, nor a miraculous encounter that suddenly erases every wound of the past. Healing is a journey—gentle, sacred, holy. And though God can heal instantly, He often chooses to heal gradually because the process itself becomes part of the transformation.

Just like a broken bone that must be set, rested, strengthened, and slowly mobilized again, the broken heart also moves through stages. Not mechanical steps, but tender seasons. Seasons shaped by God's hands. Seasons that turn hurt into wholeness, pain into purpose, and scars into testimonies.

What follows is not a psychological chart, but a spiritual journey woven throughout Scripture. You will see these stages reflected in the lives of Moses, David, Hannah, Job, Peter, Paul, and countless others whom God rebuilt slowly, beautifully, and thoroughly.

Stage 1: Honesty — Where Healing Begins

All healing begins with truth.

No restoration happens in denial. No breakthrough begins with pretending. This is why God asked Adam, "Where are you?" God knew where Adam was. But Adam needed to know where he was. Honesty is the first sacred step—the moment when a person stops running, stops hiding, and allows the light of truth into their wounded places.

David modeled this in Psalm 51 when he confessed, "Against You, and You only, have I sinned." He stopped pointing fingers, stopped justifying, stopped defending. His healing began the moment he stepped into honesty.

I once counseled a young man named *Jared*, who carried crippling anxiety. For years he hid it behind humor, busyness, and ministry involvement. But one afternoon, he whispered through tears, "I'm not okay. I can't pretend anymore." That confession did not weaken him—it opened the door to healing.

Honesty is the doorway. Honesty breaks the silence. Honesty turns the key for God to walk in.

Stage 2: Expression — Letting the Heart Speak

After honesty comes expression—giving voice to the pain we've suppressed.

Hannah expressed her anguish through silent sobs in the temple. The psalmists expressed their agony through raw poetry. Job expressed his sorrow through lament. Even Jesus expressed His agony with tears in Gethsemane and a cry on the cross.

God is not intimidated by anguish. He is not offended by tears. He is not shaken by questions. He invites us to express what hurts because unexpressed pain becomes buried pain, and buried pain becomes infected pain.

A woman named *Leena* once opened up about her abusive childhood. She had buried the memories for years, fearing that remembering would break her. But when she finally spoke—slowly, tremblingly—healing began as her secrets lost their power.

Expression is not weakness. It is worship. Because it brings our brokenness into God's presence.

Stage 3: Surrender — Letting God Take Over

Healing requires surrender—not giving up on life, but giving God permission to rebuild.

Surrender looks different for each person:

- ✓ *For David, it was repentance.*
- ✓ *For Moses, it was stepping back from self-reliance.*
- ✓ *For Peter, it was returning to Jesus after failure.*
- ✓ *For Paul, it was laying down his pride.*
- ✓ *For Hannah, it was offering Samuel to God.*

Surrender is the moment the clay stops resisting the potter's hands.

A businessman named *Suresh* battled unforgiveness for years after being betrayed by a partner. He was honest, he expressed his pain, but healing didn't begin until one night he prayed, "Lord, I can't carry this anymore. Take it." That was the moment God began softening his heart and breaking the chains of bitterness.

Surrender is not the end—it is the beginning of rebuilding.

Stage 4: Reframing — Seeing From God's Perspective

This is the stage where God begins renewing the mind. Healing is not only emotional—it is cognitive. God reshapes how we see ourselves, our wounds, our past, and even Him.

Joseph reframed his suffering when he said, "You meant it for evil, but God meant it for good." Paul reframed his thorn, realizing God's power was revealed through his weakness. Job reframed his trauma after encountering God,

saying, *"My ears had heard...but now my eyes have seen You."*
Reframing does not deny pain. It puts pain in God's context.
A divorced woman named *Annie* once told me, "I thought my story ended when my husband left. But now I see God used that breaking to rebuild me." She hadn't changed her past, but she had changed her perspective—and that changed everything.
Healing requires new lenses. Not rose-colored lenses—but redeemed ones.

Stage 5: Restoration — The Gentle Touch of God
This is the season where God actively rebuilds—where He fills the cracks with gold, strengthens the fragile places, heals old traumas, rewrites limiting beliefs, and restores identity.

- ✓ *Peter was restored by love on the seashore.*
- ✓ *Naomi was restored through Boaz and Ruth.*
- ✓ *Job was restored when God turned his captivity.*
- ✓ *David was restored through worship and repentance.*
- ✓ *Elijah was restored through rest and God's whisper.*

Restoration does not always change circumstances immediately. Restoration first changes the heart.
A mother named *Rekha*, whose son battled addiction, once told me, *"My situation hasn't changed yet... but something inside me is healed. I feel peace again."* That is restoration.
Sometimes God heals the heart before He heals the story. Sometimes He heals the story after He heals the heart. Either way, He restores.

Stage 6: Renewal — A New Spirit, A New Identity, A New Beginning

Renewal is the stage where the person becomes stronger than before.

- ✓ Where the eyes see clearer.
- ✓ Where hope replaces despair.
- ✓ Where faith becomes fire.
- ✓ Where identity becomes anchored.

This is what happened to Peter after Pentecost.

This is what happened to Paul after baptism.

This is what happened to Hannah after Samuel's birth.

This is what happened to Ruth when she married Boaz.

This is what happened to Joseph when he embraced his brothers.

Renewal is God breathing new life into old places.

A man named *Daniel*, who battled years of guilt after abandoning his family during his alcoholic years, eventually renewed his identity through counseling, repentance, and the love of Christ. He rebuilt his relationship with his children slowly, tenderly. His son later told him, "Dad, you're not who you used to be." Renewal had transformed him.

Renewal is not a return to who you were— it is becoming who God meant you to be.

Stage 7: Redeployment — Your Pain Becomes Purpose

The final stage of healing is when God takes what once broke you and uses it to bless others.

- ✓ *Joseph blessed the very brothers who hurt him.*
- ✓ *Moses delivered the people he once fled from.*

- ✓ *Paul ministered to the very church he once persecuted.*
- ✓ *Peter fed the sheep he once hid from.*
- ✓ *Naomi nurtured a new generation.*
- ✓ *David strengthened the broken-hearted through the Psalms.*

Redeployment is when God says, *"Now that you are restored, become a restorer."*

This is where your story becomes someone else's survival guide. Where your testimony becomes someone else's lifeline. Where your healed scars become someone else's hope.

A woman named *Serah*, who suffered years of domestic abuse, now leads a support group for women who feel trapped. She once cried alone, but now her story becomes the healing balm for others. God redeployed her pain into purpose.

This is the beauty of God's restoration— He heals us so that through us, He can heal others.

The Journey is Personal, But the Presence is Constant

Every person moves through these stages differently. Some move slowly. Some move quickly. Some revisit stages. Some skip stages.

But the presence of God remains the same.

He is there in honesty. He is there in expression. He is there in surrender. He is there in reframing. He is there in restoration. He is there in renewal. He is there in redeployment. Healing is not a destination. Healing is a companionship. Healing is walking with the One who rebuilds us from the inside out. Because when God heals a heart, He does not merely close wounds— He creates warriors. He does not merely repair losses—He births destinies. He does not merely restore people— He raises restorers.

And step by holy step, hurt becomes wholeness, pain becomes purpose, and broken becomes built.

When You Don't Understand God's Hand, Trust His Heart

There are seasons in life when God's actions don't make sense—moments when His silence feels louder than His promises, when prayers seem to evaporate into the sky, when suffering arrives uninvited and stays longer than expected. These are the nights when faith trembles, hearts question, and even strong believers whisper, "Lord… why me?"

Every believer eventually walks through moments when God's *hand* is hidden. It is in these seasons that God invites us to trust not what we see, but who He is. To trust His heart when His hand feels untraceable.

Isaiah 43:2 contains a truth that only brokenhearted people truly understand: "When you pass through the waters, I will be with you."

Notice God didn't say *if*, but *when*. And He didn't promise the absence of deep waters—He promised His presence *in* them. That is the foundation of trust when life doesn't make sense.

A Painful Mystery: Why the Hardest Seasons Feel Silent

One evening, a woman named *Mira* sat across from me in a counseling session. Her husband had walked out, leaving her with two small children and shattered dreams. As tears streamed down her face, she whispered the question many believers dare not say out loud: *"Pastor… why would God let this happen? Why didn't He stop it?"*

I didn't offer a theological lecture. I simply told her the truth: *"There are seasons when you won't understand God's hand. But you can always trust His heart."*

Days later, she returned—still hurting, but stronger. She said, *"I don't understand anything right now. But I think God is closer than I thought."*

That, my friend, is faith. Not understanding everything— but trusting God anyway.

The Old Testament Voice: God in the Dark Places

Many heroes of Scripture had moments when God's actions made no sense.

Abraham on Moriah

God had promised him a son, waited decades to give him Isaac, and then asked him to lay the child on an altar. Nothing about God's hand made sense. Isaac represented the promise, the future, the covenant—and God required Abraham to surrender him.

But when Abraham couldn't see God's hand, he trusted His heart: *"God will provide."*

And God did. Not a minute early. Not a minute late.

Joseph in the Prison

Joseph was betrayed by brothers, accused falsely, and forgotten in prison. He had dreams from God, yet life looked like a nightmare. But when Joseph couldn't understand God's hand, he trusted God's heart—and later testified, *"You meant evil… but God meant it for good."*

He saw what he couldn't see earlier.

Job in the Ashes

Job lost everything—children, wealth, health—and heaven went silent. Even his wife said, "Curse God and die." Yet Job, confused and hurting, clung to trust: *"Though He slay me, yet will I trust Him."*

When Job couldn't see God's hand, he leaned on God's unchanging heart.

The New Testament Echo: God in the Shadows

The New Testament is no stranger to seasons of confusion.

Mary and Martha

When Lazarus fell sick, they sent word to Jesus. But Jesus delayed. The delay confused them, disappointed them, and ultimately broke their hearts. Yet Jesus told Martha, *"Did I not tell you that if you believe, you will see the glory of God?"*

Sometimes God delays so He can reveal a deeper glory.

John the Baptist

He baptized Jesus, saw the heavens open, heard the Father speak, and proclaimed, *"Behold the Lamb of God!"* But later, imprisoned and alone, he sent disciples to ask, "Are You the one… or should we expect another?"

Even the greatest prophet had a "Why, God?" moment. Jesus didn't rebuke him. He sent reassurance.

Jesus in Gethsemane

No moment reveals this truth more painfully than Jesus Himself crying, "*My God, My God, why have You forsaken Me?"*

Even the Son felt abandoned so that you would never be.

God may be silent, but He is never absent.

The "Why Me?" Seasons

There are seasons when the hardest question in the world is simply: *"Why me?"*

A man named *Roshan* once came to me after being diagnosed with a rare illness. He wasn't angry—he was broken. His wife wept beside him. "We serve," she said. *"We pray. We give. Why would God allow this?"*

The truth is, sometimes we won't know the "why"—not on this side of eternity. But Romans 8:28 gives us an anchor strong enough to hold through any storm: *"All things work together for good to those who love God."*

Not all things *are* good. But all things *work together* for good.

- ✓ *We don't always get explanations, but we always receive presence.*
- ✓ *We don't always get answers, but we always receive assurance.*
- ✓ *We don't always understand God's plan, but we always experience God's love.*

Trusting a God Who Writes Better Stories Than You Do

One of the hardest truths to embrace is that God is writing a story bigger than your pain. He sees every chapter—past, present, and future—while we often see only a few
paragraphs.

Our life is like a tapestry viewed from the backside—knots, threads, and tangled pieces. But God sees the front. He sees the masterpiece being formed.

During a counseling session with a young widower named *Elijah*, he wept over the unexpected loss of his wife. Everything in his life collapsed in that one devastating moment. He told me, "I can't believe God has any plan left for me." Months later, as he slowly healed, he admitted something profound: *"I still don't understand everything, but I trust Him more now than ever."*

When you walk through fire, something changes.

Not God. You!
Your faith. Your depth. Your trust.
Isaiah 43:2 says *"When you walk through the fire, you shall not be burned; the flames will not set you ablaze."*
God never promised that the fire would be removed—only that *you would be preserved*.

The Heart Behind the Hand
When life hurts and heaven seems silent, here is a truth to cling to:
God's heart is always kind, even when His hand feels confusing.
You may not understand His timing.
You may not understand His decisions.
You may not understand His methods.
But never doubt His heart.
He cannot stop loving you. He cannot abandon you. He cannot forget you. He cannot fail you. Even when you don't understand His hand, you can always trust the heart that was pierced for you.

The Dark Season is Not the Last Chapter
God specializes in showing up when all seems lost:
- ✓ *When Israel was between the Red Sea and Pharaoh's army, God showed up.*
- ✓ *When Daniel was in the lions' den, God showed up.*
- ✓ *When Paul was shipwrecked, God showed up.*
- ✓ *When Peter was drowning, God showed up.*
- ✓ *When the thief on the cross was moments from death, God showed up.*

And when your heart feels crushed and confused—He will show up.

Silence is not absence. Delay is not denial. Darkness is not abandonment. You may not understand His hand, but you can always trust His heart.

The Enemy's Strategy in Brokenness

Brokenness is never just an emotional reality—it is a spiritual battlefield. Whenever a believer suffers loss, betrayal, trauma, sickness, or failure, an unseen war begins. Not the kind fought with swords or fists, but a war for the mind, identity, and destiny.

Paul writes in Ephesians 6:12, *"For we wrestle not against flesh and blood, but against principalities… powers… rulers of darkness… spiritual wickedness."*

This means that behind every lie, every attack on your worth, every assault on your identity, there is a spiritual adversary trying to distort, discourage, and ultimately destroy the image of God in you.

Brokenness becomes the moment Satan whispers the loudest.

Because he knows—

- ✓ *A broken believer is vulnerable.*
- ✓ *A wounded believer is weary.*
- ✓ *A hurting believer is searching.*

And he waits in the shadows to strike.

But the good news is this:

God does not abandon His children in the battlefield of the mind. He equips. He strengthens. He reveals truth. And He helps us stand.

The Oldest Strategy: Lies in the Shadows

Satan has no new strategies. He only recycles the same lies dressed in different language. His first weapon in Eden was deception.

When Eve stood before the tree, Satan didn't use force—he used suggestion. *"Did God really say…?"* The same whisper comes in brokenness: *"Would a loving God really let this happen?" "Are you sure God still cares?" "Maybe you deserved this pain."*

The lies feel real because pain amplifies them. Yet, they remain lies.

Elijah Under the Juniper Tree

Elijah, the fearless prophet who called fire from heaven, sat suicidal under a tree after Jezebel's threat. In that moment of exhaustion, Satan whispered, *"You are alone. It's over."*

But God gently corrected the lie: *"You are not alone. I have preserved seven thousand who have not bowed."* (1 Kings 19)

Isolation is the enemy's playground. Truth is God's rescue rope.

David in Ziklag

When David returned to Ziklag and found the city burned, his family missing, and his men ready to stone him, the enemy whispered despair. "*You have failed. Everything is lost."*

But Scripture says, *"David strengthened himself in the Lord his God."* (1 Sam 30:6) David replaced the lies with truth— and from the ashes of Ziklag came victory.

The New Testament Reality: Satan Targets the Wounded

Jesus described the enemy as "a thief" who comes to steal, kill, and destroy (John 10:10). Satan steals hope. Kills identity. Destroys destiny. Never more aggressively than when someone is broken.

Peter After Denial

After denying Jesus three times, Peter broke down in bitter tears. In those dark hours, Satan whispered, *"You are finished. You are disqualified.*" Jesus later explained, *"Satan*

has desired to sift you as wheat." (Luke 22:31)
Sifting means shaking violently—emotionally, mentally, spiritually.

But Jesus added, *"I have prayed for you."*

He prayed not that Peter would never fall—but that Peter's *faith* would not fail.

The enemy's intention was destruction. God's intention was restoration.

Paul's Thorn in the Flesh

Paul faced what he called "*a messenger of Satan*" sent to torment him (2 Cor 12:7). But even here, Satan's harassment became a tool for God's grace. God turned the enemy's strategy into strength by declaring: *"My power is made perfect in weakness."*

The enemy aims to break you. God uses the breaking to build you.

The Modern Battlefield: Lies in the Mind

During counseling sessions, I often meet people whose greatest enemy is not their past—it is the voice that speaks after the past.

A young woman named *Samira* battled severe rejection from childhood. Whenever she failed at anything, the enemy whispered, *"You are a mistake."* She believed it until she encountered the truth that she was *"fearfully and wonderfully made"* (Psalm 139:14). As she replaced the lie with truth, her identity slowly healed.

A pastor named *Reuben*, burned out and overwhelmed, believed the lie, *"You're a failure. Your ministry is done."* The enemy attacked him at the point of exhaustion. But through prayer, rest, and Scripture, God restored him—teaching him that his worth was not in his work but in his sonship.

A teenager named *Vijay* heard constant voices saying, "You'll never change. You're just like your father." These generational lies were spiritual chains. But the truth of Ezekiel 18 broke that curse: *"The soul who sins shall die"*—not the children for the father's sins.

He learned he was free to start a new legacy.

Brokenness is the soil where lies grow fastest. But it is also the place where truth heals deepest.

The Enemy's Ultimate Goal: Identity Theft

Every biblical attack on a person's life was ultimately an attack on identity.

- ✓ *Moses doubted his calling.*
- ✓ *Gideon saw himself as the least.*
- ✓ *David saw himself as unworthy.*
- ✓ *Jeremiah saw himself as too young.*
- ✓ *Peter saw himself as disqualified.*
- ✓ *Paul saw himself as the chief of sinners.*

Each time, the enemy targeted their identity. Each time, God restored their identity.

The enemy's favorite lies include:

"You are useless."

"You are unworthy."

"You are beyond repair."

"This pain will never end."

"God has abandoned you."

"You will fail again."

These are not random thoughts. They are fiery darts (Eph 6:16). They are designed to wound the mind and weaken the soul. But every lie has a truth designed to defeat it.

Defeating the Lies: Truth Replacement Therapy

Long before psychologists discovered "cognitive reframing," Scripture taught believers how to replace lies with truth.

Paul wrote, *"Take every thought captive to Christ."* (2 Cor 10:5) Meaning— Don't accept every thought. Examine it. Expose it. Replace it.

Jesus defeated Satan in the wilderness not by debate, but by declaration. Each lie was replaced with: *"It is written."* God's truth is the only antidote to Satan's deception.

When Satan says, *"You're alone,"* God says, *"I will never leave you nor forsake you."*

When Satan says, *"You're damaged goods,"* God says, *"You are a new creation."*

When Satan says, *"You're beyond repair,"* God says, *"I will restore the years the locusts have eaten."*

When Satan says, *"This is the end,"* God says, *"I know the plans I have for you."*

When Satan says, *"God doesn't care,"* God says, *"Cast your cares on Me—for I care for you."*

This is truth replacement therapy— replacing every lie of hell with the truth of heaven.

Brokenness Does Not Break You — The Devil's Lies Do

A broken heart can still beat. A broken vessel can still carry oil. A broken life can still shine brightly. Brokenness never disqualifies. Lies do. This is why Jesus said,

"You shall know the truth, and the truth shall make you free." (John 8:32)

Truth is the scalpel that removes infection. Truth is the light that dispels darkness. Truth is the voice that

silences the enemy. Truth is the foundation that rebuilds identity.
Truth is the shield that stops Satan's arrows. When truth reigns, the enemy retreats.

God Has the Final Word

Satan always speaks first— but God always speaks last. In Eden, Satan lied— but in Calvary, God finished the story. In your broken season, hell may whisper loudly, but heaven is already preparing your resurrection. Your pain is not the final voice. Your failure is not the final chapter. Your brokenness is not the final identity.
The enemy fights hardest where God is about to work the deepest. He attacks the area where your greatest calling lies dormant. He lies the loudest where God's truth is about to break through. Satan's strategy is destruction. God's strategy is restoration.
And God always wins.

What to Do When You're Broken (The Three Biblical Responses)

Brokenness is a moment of decision. It is the crossroads where a person chooses either collapse or communion, despair or dependence, bitterness or breakthrough. When life fractures your heart—through betrayal, loss, failure, sickness, injustice, or delayed answers—your response determines your recovery.

Scripture reveals three powerful responses that open the door for God to heal, rebuild, and restore. These responses are not formulas; they are lifelines. They are not rituals; they are relational responses to a God who meets His people in the darkest valleys.

When your world collapses, the Bible teaches three anchors:

Worship.

The Word.

Praise.

These are not church activities. They are survival tools. They are weapons. They are medicine for the crushed heart.

I. WORSHIP — The Cry of a Broken Spirit

Worship is not a song. Worship is surrender. Worship is the moment your pain meets God's presence. Psalm 51:17 says, *"A broken and contrite heart, O God, You will not despise."*

God never ignores broken worship. In fact, brokenness creates a depth of worship that prosperity never can.

Old Testament Illustration — Job

Job lost everything—children, wealth, health, reputation—and still Scripture says: *"Then Job arose... fell to the ground and worshiped."* (Job 1:20) Job did not worship *because* God gave. He worshiped *because* God was still God.

His worship didn't deny pain—it declared trust. And in that moment, the enemy's plan collapsed. Satan had assumed Job's worship was dependent on God's blessings. But true worship is what remains when blessings disappear.

New Testament Illustration — The Woman With the Alabaster Jar

Her life had been broken by shame, sin, and society's scorn. Yet when she entered the Pharisee's house, she brought her brokenness to the feet of Jesus. Her tears became her worship. Her past became her perfume. Her brokenness became her offering.

Jesus said, *"She has done a beautiful thing for Me."* (Mark 14:6)

Worship turns brokenness into beauty.

A Real-Life Story — Kamal's Midnight Worship

Kamal was a father whose business collapsed, leaving him drowning in debt. For months he hid from creditors, lost sleep, and nearly lost faith. One night in desperation he knelt on his living-room floor and whispered, "God, I have nothing left but my worship." He lifted his hands with trembling fingers. No music. No choir. Just tears and surrender.

Two weeks later, breakthrough began—not immediately financial, but spiritual. Peace returned. His mind calmed. His decisions became wiser. Worship rebuilt him from the inside out.

Pastors and counselors—remind the broken that worship is not a luxury. It is a lifeline. The storm may continue, but worship anchors the soul.

II. THE WORD — The Light in the Midnight Valley

When brokenness darkens your vision, God's Word becomes your compass. When confusion clouds your mind, His Word becomes your clarity. When fear whispers lies, His Word becomes your truth.

Psalm 119:50 says, *"Your word has revived me."*

Broken people often feel spiritually numb or mentally foggy. This is when the Word becomes oxygen.

Old Testament Illustration — David at Ziklag

After his city was burned and his family taken captive, David was surrounded by men who wanted to stone him. In that moment, the enemy whispered despair. But Scripture says: *"David strengthened himself in the Lord his God."* (1 Samuel 30:6)

How?

Through the Word. Through every promise God had spoken over him. Through the anointing he carried. Through the covenant God had made.

The Word became his strength. And the Word led him to pursue, overtake, and recover all.

New Testament Illustration — Jesus in the Wilderness

The Son of God Himself faced brokenness after forty days of fasting. Satan came with lies, but Jesus defeated each attack with Scripture.

Not emotion. Not experience. Not debate. Only truth.

"It is written..." That phrase is the sword every broken believer must wield.

A Real-Life Story — Maria's Healing Through the Word

Maria struggled with depression after a failed marriage. She believed the lie, *"I am discarded."* For months she cried in silence. One day she opened Isaiah 62:4 and read:
"You shall no longer be called Forsaken."
That verse became her bread, her water, her lifeline. She wrote it on her mirror, her fridge, and her phone. Slowly, the Word rewired her identity. She began to see herself as God saw her—a crown of beauty, not a life discarded.
Pastors and counselors—give broken people the Word before giving them advice. The Word never returns void. Your words may encourage, but *God's Word heals.*

III. PRAISE — The Weapon That Breaks Chains
Worship acknowledges who God is. The Word declares what God has spoken. But praise does something entirely different: Praise *breaks things*. Praise shatters atmospheres. Praise releases deliverance.
Praise is not a feeling. Praise is a weapon. Isaiah 61:3 speaks of *"the garment of praise for the spirit of heaviness."*
Which means heaviness is spiritual—and praise is the antidote.
Old Testament Illustration — Jehoshaphat's Battle
When Judah was surrounded by three powerful armies, fear overwhelmed the people. But God instructed them to send *singers* ahead of the soldiers. As they praised, confusion fell on the enemy camp. Their praise became their victory.
Praise is not the after-party of breakthrough— it's often the trigger for breakthrough.

New Testament Illustration — Paul & Silas in Prison

Their backs were bleeding. Their feet were in stocks. Their ministry seemed over. But at midnight, in the darkest place, *"Paul and Silas sang hymns unto God."* (Acts 16:25) Heaven responded. Chains broke. Doors opened. A jailer and his family were saved. Praise is not noise— it is spiritual warfare.

A Real-Life Story — Anil's Midnight Praise

Anil, once a worship leader, lost his voice after a throat infection. Doctors told him he may never sing again. For someone who lived to praise, this was devastating.

One night, unable to sleep, he whispered the words of Psalm 34: *"I will bless the Lord at all times."* His voice cracked. His throat hurt. But he praised anyway.

Months later his voice returned—not the same tone, but deeper, richer, stronger. Today, he teaches others that praise is not about sound—it is about surrender.

Pastors and counselors—teach broken people that praise lifts the soul, confuses the enemy, and prepares the atmosphere for miracles.

When You Are Broken — Do These Three, Even If You Don't Feel Like It

When your heart is shattered, you often don't *feel* like worshiping. You don't *feel* like reading the Word. You don't *feel* like praising. But healing rarely waits for your feelings.

Healing responds to your choices. Worship softens the heart. The Word strengthens the mind. Praise lifts the spirit. Together, they rebuild the believer from the inside out.

They are the three stones David used to slay Goliath. The three strands of a cord that cannot be broken. The three ingredients God uses to rebuild a crushed soul. When the broken worship, heaven leans in. When the broken read the Word, truth enters. When the broken praise, chains fall. This is how brokenness becomes breakthrough. This is how ruin becomes restoration. This is how God takes what was shattered and turns it into something glorious.

How to Help a Broken Person

No ministry on earth is more sacred—or more delicate—than caring for a broken person. Whether you are a pastor, counselor, mentor, teacher, parent, or simply a friend, you stand on holy ground when someone opens the door of their pain and invites you in.

Broken people are not problems to be solved. They are souls to be held. They are stories in progress. They are hearts that have been bruised by life, wounded by others, or crushed under the weight of their own decisions. And the one who walks beside them must walk with reverence, gentleness, and wisdom.

Jesus Himself said He came to *"bind up the brokenhearted"* (Isaiah 61:1). Every Christian who ministers to the wounded is continuing that sacred mission. But to do this well, we must understand what brokenness looks like, what it needs, what it cannot bear, and what truly helps.

The Ministry of Listening- The First Healing Touch

When Elijah fled into the wilderness, depressed and exhausted, God did not preach at him. He did not scold him. He did not push him to "be strong." Instead, God listened. He allowed Elijah to pour out his frustration, fear, and despair.

Spiritually mature people often misunderstand listening. They assume listening is passive. But listening is deeply spiritual. Listening says, *"Your story matters. Your pain matters. You matter."*

I once sat with a young man named *Rayan*, whose marriage had collapsed after years of quiet pain. He was not looking for answers—he was looking for a witness to his suffering. As he spoke through tears, he kept saying, "*I thought God didn't care.*" When he finally fell silent, I said, "*He cares. And today, I am here so you don't carry this alone.*"

Something broke inside him—not a painful break, but the beginning of healing. Listening becomes the oil that softens the hardened places, allowing truth to enter gently.

Every broken person needs at least one compassionate listener before they will ever trust a counselor, pastor, or even God again.

Listening is love.
Listening is ministry.
Listening is Christlike.

Trauma-Informed Pastoral Care- Understanding the Wounded

Many broken people are not merely sad—they are traumatized. Trauma changes how a person thinks, reacts, feels, sleeps, trusts, and relates. Trauma makes them hyper-alert, fearful, withdrawn, or easily triggered. Trauma often rewires the brain and distorts emotions.

The Bible acknowledges trauma. Elijah shook with fear under the juniper tree. Job trembled with grief. Jeremiah wept until he could weep no longer. David spoke of bones *"crushed"* and a spirit "fainting within him." Jesus Himself was *"in anguish"* in Gethsemane. Trauma needs tenderness.

A woman named *Shobha* once came for counseling after surviving years of domestic violence. For months, she flinched at loud sounds and panicked at raised voices. Telling her "You should trust God and be strong" would have been cruel. She didn't need advice—she needed safety. She needed someone who understood her journey. She needed time, patience, and love.

Trauma-informed care means:

- ✓ *You don't rush people.*
- ✓ *You don't push them to "move on."*
- ✓ *You don't spiritualize what needs healing.*
- ✓ *You don't shame them for their reactions.*

It means you understand that healing is not linear and that wounded hearts often heal slowly. Jesus said, *"A bruised reed He will not break."* Anyone caring for the broken must follow that example.

What Not to Say to a Broken Person

Some of the deepest wounds broken people carry did not come from their crisis—but from the careless words spoken after their crisis.

Job's friends sat quietly for seven days— and when they opened their mouths, everything went wrong.

Broken hearts cannot handle:

- ✓ *"You need to have more faith."* It shames their weakness and ignores their pain.
- ✓ *"Maybe this is God's punishment."* It distorts God's character and increases fear.
- ✓ *"You should be over this by now."* It condemns their pace of healing.
- ✓ *"At least it wasn't worse."* It minimizes trauma.
- ✓ *"Everything happens for a reason."* Truth—but badly timed—can crush, not comfort.

A man named *Joel*, grieving the loss of his daughter, once told me, *"The hurt was unbearable, but what hurt more were people saying it was God's will."* He

said it with tears—because pain and theology collided in the wrong way.
Broken people need presence, not pressure.
Compassion, not correction.
Comfort, not conclusions.
There is a time for truth, but never at the expense of tenderness.

The "Restoration Map" — A Way to Walk with the Broken

Every believer who journeys with a wounded soul must understand this simple but powerful framework—a guiding map, not a rigid process. It reflects the way God restores His people throughout Scripture.

1. Create Safety

Before God spoke to Elijah, He fed him, allowed him to rest, and touched him gently.
No counseling works until a person feels safe.

2. Allow Expression

Hannah poured out her soul before the Lord. So must broken people. Tears, silence, anger, fear—let it come.

3. Listen Without Judging

Jesus listened to the woman at the well without condemnation. Healing begins where judgment ends.

4. Speak Truth in Season

God corrected Elijah's distorted belief ("*You are not alone*") only *after* Elijah had expressed his pain. Truth must be timely.

5. Guide Them Toward the Word and Worship

David healed through psalms. Job healed through revelation. Broken people heal when Scripture realigns their vision.

6. Help Them Take Small Steps

God didn't send Elijah back into ministry immediately. He led him gently. Healing requires gradual rebuilding.

7. Celebrate Progress, Not Perfection

Every small victory is holy. Every step forward is a miracle.

8. Prepare Them for Redeployment

Restored people don't just survive—they serve. Like Peter, who returned stronger after restoration, broken people eventually become healers.

This map is not your invention—it is God's pattern seen throughout Scripture.

The Heart of a Restorer

Helping a broken person means becoming an image of Christ to them.

- ✓ It means standing between their pain and the lies of the enemy.
- ✓ It means holding their story without dropping it.
- ✓ It means speaking truth without crushing the soul.
- ✓ It means loving without conditions.
- ✓ It means believing that God is still at work even when they cannot see it.

You are not the healer—God is.

You are not the Savior—Christ is.

Your role is not to fix them but to accompany them.

A teenager named *Rishi*, battling addiction and despair, once told his counselor, *"I didn't change because of a sermon. I changed because someone believed I could."* Broken people heal when someone holds hope for them until they can hold it for themselves.

To be a restorer is to become a vessel of God's compassion, patience, and presence. You do not heal alone. The Holy Spirit whispers, strengthens, convicts, comforts, and guides through you. You may not see the results immediately. You may not see the full restoration. But every word spoken in love, every tear shared, every prayer whispered, every silent moment of listening is part of God's rebuilding work.

When you help a broken person, you participate in heaven's most beautiful ministry.

Restoring Broken Marriages & Families

Marriage is one of God's most sacred gifts—and one of the enemy's greatest targets. Nothing wounds the human heart more deeply than broken trust within a covenant, and nothing disrupts a home more painfully than unresolved conflict, unhealed trauma, or unspoken wounds. When a marriage breaks, the pain does not remain between the husband and wife—it spills into the children, the extended family, the community, and even the church.

Yet restoration is possible. Not because couples are strong, but because God is. Not because wounds magically disappear, but because God rebuilds what sin and suffering have shattered.

I have watched marriages on the brink of divorce experience resurrection. I have seen couples who hated each other begin to weep in each other's arms. I have seen families torn apart by betrayal walk out of my workshop holding hands. Not because of psychological techniques alone—but because God is a Master Craftsman, and His favorite project is restoring what the world calls "too far gone."

My own journey in helping broken marriages began unexpectedly. I never set out to be a marriage counselor or therapist. But during two workshops I conducted, especially for couples who had almost given up, I saw something extraordinary. I watched the Holy Spirit take years of bitterness and melt it in a single moment of honesty. I saw hardened hearts soften with just one sentence of humility. From those moments, the Lord taught me that restored marriages are not built on perfection—they are built on repentance, forgiveness, and the relentless grace of God.

Broken Homes, But God

Scripture is full of broken marriages and families—not because God failed, but because humanity did. And yet, in every one of those stories, God worked behind the scenes to heal, help, redeem, or repurpose the brokenness.

Hosea & Gomer

Perhaps no story reflects marital restoration more profoundly than Hosea's. God asked him to marry Gomer, a woman whose heart wandered. She ran after other lovers, sold herself, and eventually lost everything. But Hosea pursued her, bought her back, covered her shame, and restored her dignity.

Hosea's story isn't merely about marriage—it is about God's love for His unfaithful people. But it also reveals something else: Even the most shattered covenant can experience redemption.

Abraham & Sarah

Their marriage endured infertility, fear, laughter, impatience, and even moments of dishonesty—yet God kept them together and fulfilled His promise through them.

Joseph & His Brothers

Though not a marriage, this family experienced betrayal so deep it would have destroyed most homes. Yet God restored them, healed their wounds, and turned their pain into purpose.

Mary, Joseph & Jesus

Even the home of the Messiah began with scandal, shame, confusion, and whispered rumors. Joseph planned to leave Mary quietly. But God intervened,

healed the misunderstanding, and built a home strong enough to raise the Savior of the world.
Scripture is clear: Broken families are not disqualified from God's plans. They are His specialty.

The Workshop Experience-When God Stepped into the Room

I remember one moment during a marriage workshop so clearly it still moves me today.
A couple—let's call them *Arun & Latha*—came in barely looking at each other. Years of anger had built a silent wall. Every session was tense. But on the second day, something remarkable happened. During a simple exercise, each spouse was asked to express only one sentence: *"This is how you made me feel."*
Latha spoke first. Her voice trembled. *"When you ignored me for months, I felt invisible… like I didn't matter."* Arun's face changed. His anger melted. He whispered, *"I didn't know. I thought silence meant peace."* He broke into tears.
In that moment, the Holy Spirit filled the room. Not with drama—but with conviction, humility, and tenderness. They apologized, for the first time in years, not defensively but sincerely. By the end of the workshop, they were praying together, hand in hand.
This is what God does. He restores—not by erasing the past, but by redeeming it.

God's Method for Marital Restoration

Marital restoration is not instantaneous. God follows a consistent pattern throughout Scripture—one that applies to couples today.

1. He Exposes the Real Issue
God never heals what we hide. He gently uncovers wounds—resentment, pride, unfaithfulness, trauma, hidden habits—so He can rebuild on truth, not pretense.
2. He Softens the Heart
Restoration begins with tenderness. God breaks the hardness produced by years of hurt. He replaces defensiveness with humility, and bitterness with compassion.
3. He Reconnects the Story
Just like He reconnected Joseph with his brothers, or Hosea with Gomer, God helps couples revisit their journey—not to relive pain, but to rediscover purpose.
4. He Heals the Wound, Not Just the Symptom
The surface issue may be anger, distance, or distrust. The real issue is often deeper: insecurity, childhood trauma, unmet needs, or unconfessed sin. God heals root, not surface.
5. He Rebuilds the Covenant
God restores honor, communication, trust, intimacy, and companionship—brick by brick.
6. He Redeems the Story
Restored marriages often become testimonies. The very area where they fell becomes the area where they minister. This is the beauty of divine restoration.

Case Studies of Restored Families
Case 1: Samuel & Priya — Betrayal to Healing
Samuel had an emotional affair online. Priya discovered messages and became shattered. Their home turned cold. Trust disappeared overnight.
Through counseling, Samuel repented deeply. Priya agreed, though trembling, to begin the healing

journey. It took months—weeks of tears, painfully honest conversations, boundaries, and accountability. Slowly, trust rebuilt.

Today, they mentor young couples, using their scar as healing balm for others.

Case 2: John & Shiela — A Silent Marriage Finds Its Voice

John was raised in a home where emotions were never expressed. Shiela was deeply emotional. Years of misunderstandings created loneliness in the marriage.

Through biblical counseling, John learned to communicate, and Shiela learned to interpret his silence differently. Their marriage didn't change overnight, but both changed gradually. Today they pray together daily—a miracle neither thought possible.

Case 3: The Fernandes Family — A Home Divided by Addiction

Raj battled alcohol addiction for years. His wife, Maria, nearly left him multiple times. Their teenage son, Aaron, grew bitter and rebellious.

After a severe health scare, Raj surrendered to Christ. Recovery was slow. Counseling healed Maria's exhaustion and resentment. God restored the father-son relationship through months of intentional conversations, apologies, and forgiveness.

Their home now hosts a small prayer group—proof that God redeems what addiction tries to destroy.

Healing Family Wounds-God's Gentle Process

Family wounds often run deeper than marital wounds. A spouse hurts you today, but a parent may have wounded you twenty years ago, and that stain remains.

God heals family wounds through:

- ✓ *Honest lament, like David crying out in the Psalms.*
- ✓ *Forgiveness, like Joseph extending grace to his brothers.*
- ✓ *Restoration of identity, like the father embracing the prodigal son.*
- ✓ *Fresh beginnings, like Naomi finding joy again through Ruth and Boaz.*

Families break when communication breaks, trust breaks, or patterns of sin repeat. But families heal when grace becomes the operating system of the home.

Healing often begins with one person—a son who chooses forgiveness, a husband who chooses humility, a wife who chooses prayer, or a parent who chooses repentance.

Healing begins small, but God grows it.

Restored Marriages Become Restorers of Others

When God restores a marriage, He rarely stops with that home.

He uses that couple: to teach others, to strengthen others, to mentor younger couples, to counsel the hurting, to guide the confused, to model forgiveness, and to showcase His power.

Your restored marriage becomes someone else's survival story. Your rebuilt home becomes a lighthouse in storms. Your scars become tools in the hands of God. Marriages are not restored in heaven—they are restored on earth. Because restored marriages restore generations.

Finding Purpose After Pain: How God Uses Restored People to Heal Others

There comes a moment in every restoration journey when a person realizes something astonishing: **God never wastes pain**.

- ✓ *What once felt like the end becomes the beginning of a new calling.*
- ✓ *What once broke you becomes what God uses to build others.*
- ✓ *The very place where you bled becomes the place where you bless.*

This is not accidental—it is divine design. All throughout Scripture, God consistently uses the restored to restore, the healed to heal, and the rebuilt to rebuild.

- ✓ Pain becomes a ministry.
- ✓ Scars become testimonies. Weakness becomes strength.
- ✓ Brokenness becomes purpose.

This is the mystery of grace: God turns your greatest misery into your greatest ministry.

The God Who Recycles Pain

God is not a God who merely fixes; He re-purposes.

- ✓ He does not just heal wounds; He transforms them into wisdom.
- ✓ He does not just patch broken hearts; He makes them reservoirs of compassion.
- ✓ He does not just restore lost years; He turns them into seeds that nourish others.

This truth is written into every page of Scripture.

Old Testament Examples-Scars that Minister

Joseph — The Wounded Counselor of a Nation

Joseph was betrayed, rejected, lied about, imprisoned, forgotten. The pain was real. The brokenness was deep. Yet God took every injustice and harvested it into purpose.

In Genesis 50:20, Joseph declared, *"You meant it for evil, but God meant it for good—to save many lives."*

Joseph did not minister in spite of his pain— he ministered because of it.

- ✓ *His suffering sharpened his compassion.*
- ✓ *His betrayal taught him forgiveness.*
- ✓ *His rejection taught him resilience.*
- ✓ *His prison taught him patience.*

Pain prepared him for purpose.

Moses — The Fugitive Who Became a Deliverer

Moses fled Egypt in fear and shame. He spent 40 years in obscurity, feeling like a failure. Yet God turned the broken shepherd into a prophetic leader.

- ✓ *What broke him in Egypt built him in Midian.*
- ✓ *What humbled him in wilderness equipped him to lead millions.*

God turned his guilt into guidance, his fear into faith, his weakness into worship.

Naomi — The Bitter Widow Who Became a Blessed Mother

Naomi lost her husband, sons, home, and joy. She even renamed herself "Mara" bitter. But through Ruth's loyalty and Boaz's kindness, God restored her life.

The same Naomi who once said, *"The Lord has dealt bitterly with me,"* later held baby Obed—grandfather of David, ancestor of Christ.

Her pain became a part of God's redemptive story.

New Testament Examples-Transformed to Transform

Peter — From Failure to Foundation

Peter denied Jesus three times. His shame ran deep. But Jesus restored him on a beach with three questions of love: *"Do you love Me?" "Feed My sheep."*

- ✓ *The man who once ran from a servant girl became the preacher of Pentecost.*
- ✓ *The one who failed publicly restored others publicly.*

His weakness became his witness.

Paul — From Destroyer to Developer

Saul persecuted the church. Saul destroyed families. Saul wounded believers. But when
Saul met Jesus, everything changed.

- ✓ *The persecutor became the pastor.*
- ✓ *The destroyer became the disciple-maker.*
- ✓ *The wounder became the healer.*

Most of the New Testament came from a man who once hated Jesus.

- ✓ His pain became his preaching.
- ✓ His past became his platform.
- ✓ His brokenness became his authority.

Mary Magdalene — From Tormented to Trusted

Once oppressed by seven demons, Mary became the first to witness the risen Christ. The one healed became the one sent.

Jesus restores the broken so they can become restorers of others.

Modern Illustrations –God Still Works this Way

The Counselor Who Was Once Broken — Emily's Story

Years ago, *Emily* survived a deeply abusive marriage. After years of healing, counseling, and prayer, she began volunteering at a women's support group. Today, she leads a ministry for abused wives, and dozens have found hope because of her compassion.

She once asked me, *"Why did God allow me to walk through that nightmare?"* Years later she answered her own question: *"So I could lead others out."*

Her pain became her pulpit.

The Ex-Alcoholic Who Became a Father to Many — Daniel's Story

Daniel was once addicted, violent, and destructive. After encountering Christ, he recovered, rebuilt his family, and now mentors young men battling addiction.

He often says, *"I know their battle intimately. That's why they trust me."* His scars became bridges of empathy.

A Mother Who Lost a Child — Grace's Story

Grace lost her daughter in a tragic accident. The grief nearly crushed her. Years later, she began comforting newly bereaved mothers. Her soft words carry healing because they come from a heart that has walked the valley.

Her tears became someone else's comfort.

How Pain Births Purpose

- ✓ Pain enlarges compassion.
- ✓ Pain produces empathy.
- ✓ Pain teaches wisdom that cannot be learned in a classroom.
- ✓ Pain humbles, deepens, and purifies.

A person who has suffered carries a unique authority— not the authority of expertise, but the authority of experience.
And when God heals them, their story becomes a healing place for others.
Their testimony becomes a shelter. Their journey becomes a map. Their survival becomes someone else's strength.

When God Calls You to Minister out of Your Wounds

Many restored people hesitate to help others because they feel unworthy.
"I'm not ready."
"I'm not good enough."
"I still have scars."
"I still feel weak."
But remember:

- ✓ *God called Moses after he ran.*
- ✓ *He called Gideon while he was hiding.*
- ✓ *He called Paul despite his violent past.*
- ✓ *He restored Peter with scars still fresh.*

God does not wait for perfection. God uses your healed wounds, not your polished strengths. The scars you carry are not symbols of shame but symbols of survival. They prove God carried you through. They prove the enemy failed. They prove restoration is possible. Your scars are sermons. Your pain is a pulpit. Your healing is a ministry.

The Power of Testimony-How God Multiplies Miracles

Revelation 12:11 says, *"They overcame him by the blood of the Lamb and the word of their testimony."*
Your testimony is warfare.

Your testimony is deliverance.
Your testimony is someone else's breakthrough.
When you tell your story, chains break in others. Your transparency gives others permission to heal. Your honesty gives others courage to hope.
Hope multiplies when shared.
Healing multiplies when testified.
Restoration multiplies when modeled.

Your New Purpose: Become A Restorer

Isaiah 58:12 declares: "*You shall be called Repairer of the Breach, Restorer of Streets to Live In.*" This is not a title given to pastors alone— it is for every restored believer.

You restore by: loving the hurting, listening deeply, praying boldly, encouraging faithfully, serving quietly, testifying courageously. God does not heal you for you alone. He heals you for generations, for communities, for families, for others walking the same valley you survived. You were broken. You were rebuilt.

And now—you become the builder.

Leading a Church or Ministry of Restoration

A church is never more like Jesus than when it becomes a sanctuary for the broken. The world is filled with wounded people—those who walk into church wearing smiles that hide bruises, hearts that hide scars, and spirits that hide years of silent suffering. In such a world, the church is called not merely to preach restoration, but to *be* restoration.

Churches today often excel at programs, events, music, and teaching. But the ministry of restoration is something deeper. It is not built on lights, stages, or structures. It is built on safety, honesty, compassion, truth, humility, and the gentle, patient love of Christ. A true restoration church becomes a hospital for the hurting, a refuge for the weary, and a workshop where God's hands mend what life has shattered.

Leading such a ministry is both beautiful and heavy. Beautiful, because you get to participate in God's healing work. Heavy, because wounded souls are fragile, complex, and sacred. But if the church can truly become a place where brokenness is not judged but embraced, not hidden but healed—then heaven touches earth.

Building Safe Spaces-The Heart of a Restoration Church

A safe space is not a comfortable room. It is an atmosphere where people feel protected, honoured, and free to be real. It is where masks can fall, tears can flow, and vulnerabilities are not punished but welcomed.

The early church in Acts 2 created such an environment. They prayed together, ate together, confessed openly, shared everything, and healed community wounds with unity. Their fellowship was magnetic because it was safe. Sinners felt safe. Seekers felt safe. The broken felt safe. Safety was their evangelism.

I remember meeting a young man named *Navin*, who entered our fellowship after surviving years of rejection. He told me, *"I stopped going to church because I always felt judged. But here… I feel like I can breathe again."* He was not drawn by a sermon. He was drawn by a safe space.

The broken don't need experts—they need embrace.
They don't need perfection—they need presence.
They don't need criticism—they need compassion.

A restoration church becomes safe when leaders become listeners, when people become non-judgmental, and when the culture shifts from "fixing people" to walking with people.

Creating A "Kintsugi" Culture- Celebrating Restored Lives

Japanese Kintsugi art teaches that broken pottery is not thrown away, but restored with gold—making the restored object more beautiful than before. A Kintsugi church does the same. It celebrates restored lives openly and boldly, not hiding scars but honoring them.

The Bible itself is a Kintsugi masterpiece.

Moses was restored.
David was restored.
Peter was restored.
Paul was restored.
The woman at the well was restored.

The demoniac of Gadara was restored.
God never hid their cracks. He highlighted them. Because His glory shines through the golden seams of grace.
A restoration church must do the same—let testimonies flow freely, let scars shine like medals of mercy, let the congregation see what God has healed.
In our fellowship, I once invited *Sharon*, a woman who survived domestic violence, to share her story. Her voice trembled at first, but as she spoke of God's healing journey, something powerful happened.
People cried. People prayed. People hugged her afterward like a sister.
She later told me, *"For the first time, my scars feel holy."*
A church that hides broken stories becomes a museum. A church that honours restored stories becomes a family.

Restoration Small Groups- The Workshop of Healing

Large gatherings inspire; small groups heal. Jesus taught the masses, but He discipled twelve. He preached publicly, but He restored personally.
A restoration small group becomes a place where:

- ✓ *Painful memories are shared without fear,*
- ✓ *Addictions are confessed without shame,*
- ✓ *Trauma is processed without judgment,*
- ✓ *Scripture becomes medicine,*
- ✓ *Prayer becomes oxygen,*
- ✓ *Community becomes therapy.*

I once led a small group for men battling hidden addictions. One of them, *Samuel*, said on the first day, *"I've never told anyone what I'm about to share."*

He confessed with trembling. Others nodded with empathy. And healing began.

These groups often become more powerful than sermons, because they are relational, honest, consistent, and safe. Many miracles happen—not through organized events, but through ten people sitting in a circle, holding each other's stories gently.

Small groups become Kintsugi workshops—where God pieces shattered hearts back together, one vulnerable conversation at a time.

Ministry Ethics-The Holiness of Counseling the Broken

Not everyone who loves God understands how to handle wounded souls safely. Good intentions are not enough. Even pastors can harm unintentionally. Broken people must be shepherded with ethics, integrity, and wisdom.

Biblical counseling requires:

- ✓ *Confidentiality, because secrets are sacred.*
- ✓ *Boundaries, because emotions can blur lines.*
- ✓ *Honor, because every person carries God's image.*
- ✓ *Humility, because we are not the healer—God is.*
- ✓ *Discernment, because some wounds require professional help.*
- ✓ *Purity, because vulnerability must never be exploited.*
- ✓ *Accountability, because ministers are human too.*

Jesus modeled perfect ethics. He protected the woman caught in adultery. He restored Peter privately before commissioning him publicly. He healed the leper with a touch something no one else dared to do. He never shamed, never manipulated, never minimized pain.

A pastor or counselor must follow His example: to guide, not to control;

- ✓ To listen, not to dominate;
- ✓ To lead gently, not forcefully;
- ✓ To heal, not to hurt.

A restoration ministry must never tolerate spiritual abuse, emotional manipulation, or unhealthy dependency. Jesus never made people dependent on Him—He empowered them to walk in freedom.

- ✓ *True ministry lifts burdens, not adds to them.*
- ✓ *True ministry restores dignity, not crushes it.*
- ✓ *True ministry mirrors the Father's heart.*

The Restoration Leader-A Human Vessel of Divine Compassion

To lead a restoration church is to become a compassionate shepherd. You do not need to be flawless. You do not need a counseling degree. But you must have a tender heart, a listening spirit, and a willingness to walk slowly with the wounded.

Leaders who restore understand:

- ✓ *That healing takes time,*
- ✓ *That relapse does not mean failure,*
- ✓ *That counselling is not fixing but accompanying,*
- ✓ *That broken people need grace more than advice,*
- ✓ *That every person is a long-term investment.*

A restoration leader becomes a living testimony of God's character. People don't follow the leader's sermons—they follow the leader's heart.

One young woman, *Myra*, who had attempted suicide years earlier, said something I will never forget: *"I didn't come back to church because someone preached. I came back because someone cared."*

That is restoration leadership. Not charisma—compassion. Not perfection—presence.

Not performance—Christlikeness.

When a Church Becomes a Home for the Broken

When a church embraces restoration as its identity, something miraculous happens:

- ✓ *Addicts find freedom.*
- ✓ *Broken marriages heal.*
- ✓ *Trauma victims find safety.*
- ✓ *The lonely find family.*
- ✓ *The ashamed find acceptance.*
- ✓ *The wounded find purpose.*
- ✓ *The depressed find hope.*
- ✓ *The rejected find belonging.*
- ✓ *The distant find God again.*

A restoration church becomes a soft place for hard stories and a holy place for divine healing. It reflects the heart of the Good Shepherd who leaves the ninety-nine for the hurting one.

Such a church is not easy to build, but it is powerful. Not flashy, but transformational. Not perfect, but deeply Christlike. When the church becomes a Kintsugi community— where cracks are not hidden, where scars are honored, where grace fills the gaps— then the world will look at us and say, *"This is what Jesus looks like."*

The Five Signs Someone Is Ready for Restoration

Restoration is not something we force on people. It is something God awakens within them. Pastors and trainers often feel pressured to "fix" a person quickly—but hearts heal only when they are ready. Restoration is a divine partnership: God initiates, the individual responds, and we join the journey with discernment.

Not everyone who is broken is ready for rebuilding. Some are still blaming, hiding, resisting, or numbing their pain. Others are in denial. Still others are crying out for transformation but don't know how to begin. One of the greatest gifts a minister can cultivate is the ability to discern the heart posture of someone standing at the threshold of healing.

Through Scripture, human stories, and years of walking with wounded people, one truth has become clear: God restores hearts that want Him more than relief, truth more than ease, and change more than comfort.

Below are five unmistakable signs—biblical and practical—that someone is finally ready to be restored.

I. HUMILITY — The Doorway God Always Walks Through

Humility does not mean weakness. It means softness. It means the heart has stopped fighting God and started yielding to Him.

The proud cannot heal because they will not bow. But the humble become God's favorite students.

Biblical Example: King Manasseh

Manasseh was one of Israel's most wicked kings—idol worship, bloodshed, rebellion. But when he was taken captive and chained in Babylon, Scripture says, *"He humbled himself greatly before the God of his fathers"* (2 Chronicles 33:12). Only then did God restore him.

God does not heal the defensive. But He runs toward the humble.

Real-Life Illustration: Reuben's Return

Reuben had destroyed his marriage through an affair. For months he justified himself, blamed his wife, and refused responsibility. Nothing changed.

One evening he walked into my office, dropped to his knees, and said, *"Pastor, I have sinned. I don't deserve mercy. But I want to change."*

That was the moment restoration began. His humility unlocked what months of arguments never could. A humble heart is a heart ready for God.

II. HONESTY — The Courage to Tell the Truth to God and Self

Broken people often hide behind excuses, masks, or selective truth. But true healing begins the moment they step into radical honesty—not just with the counselor, but with themselves and with God.

David's restoration began not when Nathan rebuked him, but when David said, *"I have sinned against the Lord."*

The truth does not destroy a person—it delivers them. Honesty doesn't weaken them— it awakens them.

Biblical Example: The Prodigal Son

He did not begin his journey home when he left the pigs. He began it when he said,

"I have sinned... I am no longer worthy." That confession was the first step in redemption.

Real-Life Illustration: Sarah's Secret

Sarah carried a secret addiction for years. She attended church faithfully, but inwardly battled shame. Her breakthrough came when she finally confessed in a safe counseling session, "*This is who I have become, and I need help.*"

Her healing moved faster than she expected because honesty opens spiritual arteries. You cannot heal what you do not reveal.

When a person becomes honest—brutally, beautifully honest—God immediately draws near.

III. HUNGER — A Deep Desire to Change, Grow, and Live Differently

Hunger is the spark of restoration. It is the longing, the ache, the holy dissatisfaction that whispers, "There has to be more than this."

Some come to pastors wanting relief, not change. But those who hunger for transformation become unstoppable.

Biblical Example: Blind Bartimaeus

Bartimaeus wasn't passive. He cried out. He pushed through crowds. He refused to be silenced. Jesus responded to his hunger, not just his need.

"There were many blind people in Israel—but only one refused to shut up."

Real-Life Illustration: Daniel's Desire

Daniel, a young believer battling pornography, attended every session, took notes, prayed, asked questions, changed routines, memorized Scripture, and sought accountability. His hunger for purity brought rapid breakthrough.

Hunger is not emotion—it is pursuit. It is evidence the Holy Spirit is stirring the heart. It is one of the loudest signs that restoration is at hand.

IV. ACCOUNTABILITY — Willingness to Walk with Others Instead of Alone

Restoration is rarely a solo journey. God restores within community. A person ready for restoration welcomes correction, guidance, and accountability.

Someone refusing accountability is not ready for change—they are ready for comfort.

Biblical Example: Saul vs. David

Saul rejected Samuel's correction and remained broken. David embraced Nathan's correction and was restored. Restoration requires teachability.

The Early Church Example

Believers "confessed their sins to one another" (James 5:16). This was not shame—it was spiritual strategy.

Real-Life Illustration: Anita's Circle

Anita, a divorced mother healing from trauma, joined a restoration small group and allowed three mature women to walk with her. She would say, *"Alone I fall. With them, I rise."*

Her willingness to submit to guidance accelerated her healing tenfold.

A person ready for restoration understands: *"I cannot rebuild myself alone."*

V. SURRENDER — Letting God Take the Pen and Rewrite the Story

Restoration is impossible without surrender. Not partial surrender. Not conditional surrender. But full, trusting, yielded surrender.

Surrender is when the heart stops saying, *"Fix this, God,"* and starts saying, *"Change me, God."*

Biblical Example: Isaiah in the Temple

After his brokenness overwhelmed him, he cried, *"Here am I, send me."*

Surrender turned his despair into destiny.

Jesus in Gethsemane

The greatest restoration in history—our salvation—began with surrender:

"Not my will, but Yours be done."

Real-Life Illustration: Kamala's Release

Kamala held unforgiveness toward her sister for years. Her bitterness poisoned her. One day, during a counseling session, she sighed deeply and said, *"I'm tired of carrying this. Lord, I surrender."*

From that moment onward, healing unraveled like a long, tangled thread finally freed.

Surrender is not losing—it is winning through God.

When these Five Signs Emerge- Restoration has Begun

Pastors and trainers must understand these signs not to judge, but to discern readiness. A heart showing humility, honesty, hunger, accountability, and surrender is fertile soil.

God's rain falls easily there.

Transformation moves swiftly. Breakthrough becomes natural. Restoration becomes inevitable.

People who possess these qualities heal deeper, faster, and stronger. Their testimonies shine brighter. Their future becomes clearer. Their past loses power. When God sees these five signs, Heaven moves. Angels lean forward. Grace flows freely. The Holy Spirit works gently but powerfully. And a new chapter begins. Not because the person is strong—but because the person is yielded.

Restoration is not for the perfect. It is for the willing. And willingness is the soil of miracles.

The Beauty of Scars

Scars are strange things. They are the silent storytellers of our lives—proof that we were wounded, but also proof that we healed. A scar is the place where the pain once lived but no longer rules. It is the mark that says, *"God brought me through."* And yet, so often, we hide our scars as if they are stains of shame instead of signs of grace.

But heaven sees scars differently. Heaven calls scars beautiful.

One of the most profound truths about Jesus after the resurrection is this: He rose in glory, but He kept His scars. He could have emerged with flawless, untouched skin. He could have erased every evidence of the nails and the spear. But He didn't. Why? Because the scars told the story of love. The scars were His testimony.

In this chapter, we explore how God turns our wounds into witness, how scars become symbols of strength, and why the broken but healed heart is one of the most powerful tools God uses on earth.

I. The Scars of Jesus: Proof That Love Suffers and Still Wins

After the resurrection, Jesus appeared to His disciples who were trembling behind locked doors, unsure of what to believe. Thomas, overwhelmed with doubt, declared that he would not believe unless he saw and touched the scars for himself.

Jesus responded not with anger but with invitation: *"Put your finger here; see my hands. Reach out your hand and put it into my side."* — John 20:27

He didn't hide His scars. He exposed them as evidence of victory. Those scars were not reminders of defeat—they were reminders of redemption. They did not represent the brutality of the cross—they represented the beauty of resurrection.

The scars preached a sermon Thomas needed to hear: *"Your wounds do not disqualify you. They qualify you for grace."*

If the Savior of the world did not erase His scars, why should we be ashamed of ours?

II. Scars in the Old Testament: Marks That Tell a Story

Throughout Scripture, healed wounds become holy testimonies.

Jacob's Limp

Jacob wrestled with God and came away with a permanent limp (Genesis 32:31). It was a scar of sorts—a physical reminder of a spiritual encounter. Every step Jacob took after that night whispered: *"I am not who I used to be. God changed me."*

His limp wasn't shameful—it was sacred. It told the world that God had touched him.

Joseph's Wounds Turned Wonders

Joseph carried invisible scars—betrayal from brothers, false accusation, years in prison. Those inner scars could have made him bitter. Instead, they became the foundation of his calling. When he finally faced his brothers, he said: *"You meant evil against me, but God meant it for good."* — Genesis 50:20

- ✓ *His scars became wisdom.*
- ✓ *His scars became perspective.*
- ✓ *His scars became compassion for others.*
- ✓ *His scars became the reason entire nations were fed during famine.*

Scars don't end your story—they deepen it.

III. Scars in the New Testament: Redemption Written on Skin

Paul's Marks of Ministry

Paul wrote something striking in Galatians 6:17: *"I bear on my body the marks of the Lord Jesus."*

He wasn't speaking figuratively. He literally carried scars from beatings, stonings, lashes, shipwrecks, imprisonments. Those scars spoke louder than sermons. They proved he did not merely preach the gospel—he lived it, suffered for it, and loved through it.

Paul's scars were his credentials.

The Woman with the Alabaster Jar

Though she is unnamed, her past left scars on her heart—scars of rejection, shame, and sin. Yet when she wept at Jesus' feet, those scars became testimonies of forgiveness. Jesus said of her: *"Her many sins have been forgiven—as her great love has shown."* — Luke 7:47

Her healed scars produced extravagant worship.

IV. Real-Life Story: Miriam's Marriage Scar

Miriam had lived through a devastating marriage collapse. Her husband walked out after twenty-three years, leaving her with two children and a mountain of debt. The pain cut her deeply. For months she hid from everyone, ashamed of what people would say.

But healing came slowly—through counseling, prayer, community support, and personal surrender.

Years later, Miriam began mentoring young wives in her church who were facing marital struggles. One young woman named *Priya* asked her, *"How do you know exactly what I am feeling?"*

Miriam smiled gently and replied, *"Because I have walked through this valley. And God walked with me."*

Her scar became her ministry. The wound that once almost destroyed her became the very place God used her the most.

V. Real-Life Story: Samuel's Battle with Addiction

Samuel had been addicted to alcohol for fifteen years. His wife *Nisha* had prayed until her tears dried up. When he finally hit rock bottom, he entered a recovery program where he met Christ in a dramatic encounter.

Five years later, he now leads a support group for men battling addiction. His testimony—raw, honest, scarred—breaks chains in others. Men listen to him because he doesn't speak theory; he speaks from healed wounds.

He often tells them, *"I am not proud of the scars, but I am grateful I survived them."*

And every man in that room sees hope. God uses scars that have been surrendered to Him.

VI. Scars Are Not Signs of Shame — They Are Signs of Survival

A scar announces, *"The wound is closed. The bleeding has stopped. The infection has passed. Life has continued."*

Scars whisper:

"You survived what tried to kill you."

"You endured what others did not see."

"You walked through fire and came out alive."

Scars are not stains on your story; they are signatures of God's mercy. Shame hides scars. Grace reveals them. Testimony celebrates them.

- ✓ *If Jacob could limp,*
- ✓ *If Joseph could forgive,*
- ✓ *If Paul could boast in his marks,*
- ✓ *If Jesus could keep His scars— then we, too, can embrace ours.*

VII. Scars Become Lamps for Others Walking in Darkness

When you refuse to hide your scars, you become a lighthouse. God shines through the very places you once tried to conceal.

- ✓ *Parents, your healed scars become wisdom for your children.*
- ✓ *Counselors, your scars become empathy for your counselees.*
- ✓ *Pastors, your scars become messages that carry weight.*
- ✓ *Leaders, your scars become bridges of trust.*

God never wastes a wound. He transforms it into a tool.

Your scar may be the exact story someone else needs to hear so they can believe their healing is possible.

VIII. God Does Not Heal You to Hide You — He Heals You to Use You

The enemy wants you to believe your scars make you less valuable. God says they make you more usable. The enemy wants you to bury your past. God wants to redeem it. The enemy wants you to pretend nothing happened. God wants you to proclaim what He has done. This is the kingdom paradox: What the enemy used to break you, God uses to build you. Your scars are sermons written on your skin.

IX. The Most Beautiful Scar in Scripture

One day, when we see Jesus face to face, He will still have the scars. They will forever declare: *"My love cost Me everything. And you were worth it."* Which means our scars, too, will carry glory. Not shame. Not guilt. Not regret. But glory. Scars become beautiful when God becomes the storyteller.

You Are a Kintsugi Masterpiece

There is a breathtaking moment in the Kintsugi process when the broken pottery—once shattered, discarded, seemingly useless—begins to take shape again under the hands of the master craftsman. The fragments are carefully gathered. The sharp, jagged edges are gently dusted. The cracks are not hidden or glued in secret. They are intentionally filled with gold.

Not just restored… Not just repaired… But made more beautiful *because* of the break.

This is the heart of God toward us.

He does not hide your broken past—He highlights it with healing. He does not erase your scars—He fills them with grace. He does not discard you because of your weakness—He transforms your weakness into the very place His strength shines the brightest.

You are not a repaired vessel. You are a Kintsugi masterpiece in the hands of the God who makes all things new.

I. God Highlights—He Does Not Hide—Your Broken Past

Most of us grow up learning to hide our pain. We hide our failures, our addictions, our shame, and our wounds. We build masks to look stronger than we are. We avoid conversations that might expose our past. We worry about what people will say if they *"know too much."*

But God does not work behind masks. He works through cracks. Jesus did not hide His scars after the resurrection. He showed them to Thomas (John

20:27). His scars became proof of power, not weakness.

Biblical Example: The Woman at the Well

In John 4, Jesus meets a Samaritan woman whose life is filled with relational scars. Her past is broken. Her reputation is shattered. Yet what does Jesus do?

He exposes, then heals.

He reveals, then redeems.

He uncovers, then restores.

And what does this woman do after encountering the Messiah? She runs back to her village shouting, *"Come, see a man who told me everything I ever did!"* — John 4:29

The very past she once hid became the testimony that brought revival to her village.

God did not erase her story. He rewrote it.

II. Every Crack Filled With Grace

Paul once begged God to remove his *"thorn,"* a painful weakness that constantly reminded him of his limitations. God didn't remove it. Instead, He said something that forever changed how we understand brokenness: *"My grace is sufficient for you, for My strength is made perfect in weakness."* — 2 Corinthians 12:9

Perfect strength through imperfect people. This is Kintsugi. God fills the cracked places with gold.

Biblical Example: Rahab

Her past was dark. Her reputation shameful. But Hebrews 11 lists her among heroes of faith. Why? Because God filled her cracks with redemption. A woman once broken by sin became part of the genealogy of Christ Himself (Matthew 1:5).

Biblical Example: Peter

His denial was a deep crack, a moment of failure that could have defined him. Instead, Jesus restored him with grace and turned him into a rock of the early church.

Real-Life Story: Arun the Addict

Arun had been addicted to drugs for years. His parents disowned him. His marriage collapsed. His body bore scars of overdose attempts. When he finally encountered Christ in a rehab ministry, he kept saying, *"I am too broken to be used."*

But today, he is a counselor for youth battling addiction. Every session begins with the same line:

"I know the darkness you feel. I once lived there myself."

His cracks became his credibility.

His weakness became his ministry.

His brokenness became his calling.

God filled every fracture with gold.

III. God Makes All Things New—Even the Parts You Think Are Beyond Repair

In Revelation 21:5, Jesus declares, *"Behold, I make all things new."*

He does not say, "I make all new things." but "I make all things new."

He doesn't discard your past. He transforms it.

He doesn't erase your story. He rewrites it with redemption ink.

He takes the very places you were humiliated, rejected, wounded, or scarred, and He turns them into places of revelation and ministry.

Biblical Example: Moses

His anger, insecurity, and murder filled him with guilt. But God did not erase Moses' past—He redeemed it.

Moses' deepest fear ("I am not eloquent") became the very place God displayed His power.

Biblical Example: Naomi

She returned to Bethlehem bitter, empty, grieving, and broken. But the same woman who said, "Call me Mara" (meaning bitter) became the grandmother of Obed, the ancestor of David and Christ.

God took her grief and wove it into salvation history.

IV. Real-Life Story: Anjali's Kintsugi Journey

Anjali had grown up in a violent home. Her father was an alcoholic who beat her mother almost weekly. She swore she would never forgive him. For years, she hid her past from her church friends, pretending her family was stable.

But the day she found healing in Christ, God whispered to her heart: *"Your story is someone's survival guide."*

Slowly, courage replaced shame. She started sharing her testimony with teenage girls from similar homes. Today, she leads a support ministry for abused women.

The cracks she once hid are now filled with pure gold of God's grace. She is a Kintsugi masterpiece.

V. You Are Proof of a God Who Restores

Your story is not a story of perfection—it is a story of redemption. Your testimony is not flawless—it is Spirit-filled.

Your journey is not straight—it is shaped by the hands of a God who bends brokenness into beauty.

Kintsugi teaches us: *The value of the vessel increases after the repair.*

You are more valuable today—not less—because of what God healed in you.

Your past may explain you, but it does not define you.
Your scars may tell your story, but grace tells the ending.
You are not marked by failure. You are marked by restoration.
You are not a broken vessel discarded on the ground. You are a masterpiece lifted by the Master.
You are not a hopeless case. You are a living testimony.
And you are not forgotten. You are individually, intentionally, lovingly restored by God Himself.

VI. God Is Not Ashamed of Your Cracks—He Works Through Them

Some believers think they must be perfect to be used. But God does not require perfection. He requires permission.
He waits for your surrender, your honesty, your willingness to let Him fill the cracks.
Because the places where you were once shattered become the places where His glory shines brightest.
You are not just restored. You are redeemed. You are repurposed. You are radiant.
You are a Kintsugi masterpiece held together by the gold of grace.

Broken for Revival

Revival does not begin in stadiums. It does not start with smoke machines, large choirs, or eloquent sermons. It does not ignite because of polished programs or perfect people. Revival begins where something breaks. Where pride breaks. Where self-sufficiency breaks. Where the heart bows low before God.

The greatest move of God always begins in the most unexpected place— inside a broken vessel.

God has never used the proud to awaken nations. He has never used the self-righteous to heal the wounded. He has never used the independent to bring down His glory.

God's revivalists—through Scripture and history—were always those whose hearts had been cracked open and filled with humility, surrender, and holy desperation.

This is why the Psalmist wrote: "*The sacrifices of God are a broken spirit; a broken and a contrite heart, O God, You will not despise.*" — Psalm 51:17

If the beginning of revival had a sound, it would be the sound of a heart breaking before God.

I. Why God Uses Only Broken People

A broken vessel leaks.

And that is exactly what God desires—people who leak grace, leak compassion, leak humility, leak love, leak mercy, leak the fragrance of Christ wherever they go. God cannot pour His fire into a heart that is full of itself. He pours into hearts that are emptied… because brokenness creates capacity.

Biblical Example: Isaiah's Breaking Before His Calling

Isaiah wasn't commissioned when he saw the throne. He wasn't sent when he saw the angels. He was sent when he cried, *"Woe is me! For I am undone!"* — Isaiah 6:5

Undone means *"broken, unravelled, exposed, nothing left to boast about."*

Once Isaiah shattered, God said, *"Now whom shall I send?"* Heaven waits for brokenness before releasing assignments.

Biblical Example: Moses in the Wilderness

Moses was brilliant, trained, powerful—but unusable. It wasn't until he was broken in Midian, stripped of anger, pride, and self-reliance, that God called him to lead Israel. God did not use the prince. He used the broken shepherd. Brokenness aligns us with heaven.

II. Revival is the Overflow of Broken Vessels

Revival is not an event; it is an overflow. The Spirit pours into a broken vessel until that vessel spills over into homes, churches, communities, and nations.

God never begins revival with crowds—He begins it with one person on their knees.

Biblical Example: Hannah's Revival

Before Samuel—before the prophetic awakening of Israel—there was a broken woman in the temple weeping her heart out. Her anguish became the birthplace of revival.

Hannah's brokenness before God produced Samuel, and Samuel produced a spiritual awakening in the nation. It always starts with one broken heart.

Biblical Example: The Disciples Before Pentecost

Pentecost did not descend upon proud leaders. It came upon a group of men who had recently failed

Jesus, mourned their betrayal, confessed their fear, and gathered in humility. Their brokenness became the womb of the Holy Spirit's fire.

God can revive a city. But first, He revives a person.

III. Real-Life Story: When One Broken Woman Changed a Community

Rekha was known in her village for her violent husband, poverty, and constant sorrow. She attended a small prayer meeting one evening, sitting at the back, eyes swollen from crying. The pastor didn't preach a powerful sermon that day—he simply asked, *"Who needs Jesus to touch the deepest wound?"*

Rekha broke. She wept until she had no strength left. Her surrender filled the small room like fragrance.

Weeks later, neighbors began noticing changes—her voice softened, her fear dissolved, and she prayed with a new authority. Soon people from her street began asking her to pray for them.

Within a year, twelve families had come to Christ. Today, there is a thriving house fellowship in that village. It all began with one broken heart becoming a doorway for revival.

IV. Real-Life Story: Broken Youth, Burning Fire

Joel, once a drug addict, walked into a youth meeting only because a friend forced him. During worship, he suddenly knelt, sobbing uncontrollably. He later said, *"It felt like my chest broke open."*

That night, he experienced a drastic transformation. His brokenness led to intense hunger for God. He started a small Bible study in his college canteen. Within months, that group grew to 80 students. Several received Christ. Many were healed. A few joined ministry. Joel often says, *"I didn't bring revival. My brokenness did."*

V. Brokenness Is the Fuel of Revival

Pride quenches revival.

Performance quenches revival.

Programs without presence quench revival.

But brokenness accelerates revival like oil feeding a flame.

Biblical Example: David's Revival After Repentance

Psalm 51 was written after David's darkest sin. Only after he broke before God did revival flow again through his leadership. In the very same psalm he says: "*Then will sinners be converted unto You.*" — Psalm 51:13

David understood something profound— personal brokenness precedes national awakening. Revival begins in the repentant heart.

Biblical Example: Nineveh

Jonah preached only a simple message, *"Repent."* He didn't want revival. He didn't even preach passionately. But the people responded with brokenness—sackcloth, fasting, crying out. And God spared an entire city.

It wasn't Jonah's sermon that changed Nineveh. It was Nineveh's brokenness that changed the city.

VI. God Breaks Us to Bless Others Through Us

God uses you most powerfully in the very place where you were once most broken.

- ✓ *Your testimony is your anointing.*
- ✓ *Your wounds become your wisdom.*
- ✓ *Your tears become your intercession.*
- ✓ *Your scars become your ministry.*

Biblical Example: Peter After His Denial

Before his failure, Peter was impulsive, bold, self-confident. But after he was broken by his denial, Jesus restored him—and that broken man preached a sermon that led 3,000 souls to salvation.

Peter's brokenness birthed revival. His failure became fuel for fire.

VII. What Revived People Look Like

People who have been broken and healed carry an unmistakable fragrance. You recognize them not by eloquence, but by tenderness. Not by strength, but by surrender. Not by charisma, but by compassion.

A revived person:

- ✓ *Kneels easily*
- ✓ *Forgives quickly*
- ✓ *Loves deeply*
- ✓ *Serves silently*
- ✓ *Repents willingly*
- ✓ *Worships wholeheartedly*

Because they know where God found them, and they never forget who healed them.

VIII. When Broken Hearts Cry, Heaven Answers

The history of revival—biblical and modern—is a history of pain turned into prayer, weakness turned into worship, surrender turned into supernatural fire.

You never see revival start with applause. It always starts with tears.

When a heart breaks for God, God pours Himself into that heart.

When a church breaks in repentance, God visits that church.

When a family breaks in surrender, God fills that home with His presence.

When a community breaks before Him, God sends revival.

The greatest moves of God are born through broken hearts. Because God is closest to the broken: *"The Lord is near to the brokenhearted..."* — Psalm 34:18

Brokenness attracts God.

Surrender moves Him.

Contrition invites Him.

And revival rests where pride dies.

IX. You Are God's Revival Vessel

You do not need to be perfect to be used by God. You need to be broken enough to let Him in. Your brokenness is not your handicap—it is your gateway to anointing. You are not too damaged. You are not too late. You are not too shattered. You are not too flawed. You are exactly the kind of vessel God uses when He wants to pour Himself out.

Revival is not something you watch. Revival is something you become.

You—yes, you—can be the spark God uses to set hearts on fire.

All He needs is your brokenness, placed in His hands.

From Brokenness to Building Others

There comes a moment in every believer's journey—the moment when healing is no longer only about personal restoration. It becomes about participation. Ministry. Influence. Overflow. Helping others find the same Jesus who rescued you, rebuilt you, and transformed you from the inside out.

Brokenness is not the end of the story. It is the beginning of a calling.

God never heals a person for them to keep the healing to themselves.

He restores them so they can become restorers.

He comforts them so they can comfort others.

He rescues them so they can become rescuers.

This is the divine pattern woven through Scripture and human experience:

Those who have been rebuilt by God inevitably become builders of people.

And the moment a believer realizes this, their brokenness finds purpose, and their story becomes a tool in the hand of God.

I. Your Ministry Story — When Brokenness Became a Blueprint

My own story is evidence of this divine pattern. I never planned to minister to broken people. I never imagined that my strange childhood habit of picking up broken radios, discarded typewriters, damaged speakers, and shattered guitar parts would one day become a prophetic reflection of ministry.

Back then, I only knew the thrill of restoration—of watching a useless object breathe again.

I did not know God was training my heart to see

value where others saw waste. Years later, when the little home church began unexpectedly filling with individuals from the nearby slum—wives battered by drunken husbands, children abandoned by parents, young men trapped in addiction—I realized something startling:

My heart naturally moved toward the broken because God had shaped me that way long before I knew.

It was not a ministry I pursued. It was a ministry that pursued me.

I still remember *Lakshmi*, a young mother whose husband spent every rupee on alcohol. She would come to the tiny living-room service with bruises she tried hiding behind her shawl. Every Sunday she sat quietly, head down, but her spirit soaked every word. Over time, God began healing her from the inside. One evening she came with a testimony that shook all of us: her husband had prayed with her for the first time in their marriage.

Something had rebuilt inside her—and her healing began rebuilding her home.

There is no greater joy than watching the broken become builders of others.

This is the heart of God.

II. Every Believer Is Called to Rebuild Others

Some think only pastors or trained counselors are "qualified" to help the broken. But Scripture completely disagrees. God is not looking for professional builders—He is looking for willing ones.

Isaiah 61:1–4 — The Blueprint of Every Believer's Ministry

Isaiah 61 is not written for a select few. It is the ministry DNA of every follower of Christ.

"The Spirit of the Lord is upon Me to bind up the brokenhearted… to comfort all who mourn… to rebuild the ancient ruins… to restore the places long devastated…" —Isaiah 61:1–4

Broken hearts. Ruined places. Devastated lives. Generational wounds. God sends *His people* to rebuild them.

Notice the sequence: *God heals you → God fills you → God sends you.*

You do not need a pulpit.

You do not need a title.

You do not need degrees.

You simply need a healed heart willing to help heal others.

The kingdom of God advances through rebuilt people rebuilding people.

III. God Uses Your Scars to Build Someone Else's Strength

The most powerful ministry tool you possess is not your knowledge—it is your story.

Not your ability—it is your authenticity.

Not your perfection—it is your scars.

Biblical Example: Joseph

Joseph's betrayal, false accusations, and imprisonment were his deepest wounds. But those same wounds became the wisdom he used to save nations.

His suffering qualified him to lead.

His scars became his strategy.

He told his brothers: *"God sent me ahead of you to preserve life."* — Genesis 45:5

He could preserve life *because he had known pain.*

Biblical Example: Peter

Peter's denial nearly destroyed him. But after Jesus restored him, that scar became the very place of his supernatural boldness.

The man who once cowered before a servant girl stood before thousands and declared salvation in Christ. His failure birthed his fire.

Biblical Example: Paul

Paul's broken past—persecuting believers, overseeing violence—became the story he used again and again to preach grace.

His wounds gave him a message.

His past gave him power.

His brokenness made him believable.

IV. Real-Life Story: Tara, the Builder of Women

Tara was a woman shattered by domestic abuse. Her husband abandoned her with two young daughters. For years she lived in fear and humiliation. When she encountered Christ, the healing journey was slow—filled with tears, counseling sessions, prayer, and long nights of wrestling with worthlessness.

Years later, healed but not hardened, Tara joined a small team that helped women rescued from abusive marriages. She led prayer sessions, listened for hours, and shared her own story with quiet strength.

One day a young wife whispered, *"Ma'am, how do you understand exactly how I feel?"*

Tara responded, *"Because I once lived in that darkness. But God rebuilt me, and now I will walk with you as He rebuilds you."*

The broken had become the builder.

The wounded had become the warrior.

The healed had become a healer.

V. Real-Life Story: David, the Youth Restorer

David had a terrible past—drugs, gang involvement, and juvenile detention. It was in prison that he encountered Christ. The guards noticed how he changed—no more fights, no more rage, just a young man devouring Scripture.

After release, he became part of a church that believed in second chances. Soon, David started a weekly small group for troubled boys in the community. He taught them how to pray, how to control anger, how to study, how to break addictions.

One night, one of the boys asked, *"Why do you care about us?"*

David replied, *"Because once someone cared about a boy like me."*

When God rebuilds a man, He rebuilds nations through him.

VI. Trainers and Coaches: Your Calling Is Holy

If you are a counselor, trainer, pastor, teacher, or coach, your assignment is not technical—it is spiritual. You are helping God rebuild lives.

Three sacred truths shape this calling:

1. You Are a Co-Builder With God

You are not the healer—God is. But He invites you to hold the tools. He trusts you with the fragile pieces of someone's soul.

2. You Are a Carrier of the Anointing of Isaiah 61

Whether you train in classrooms, offices, homes, or churches, you are carrying spiritual oil to the brokenhearted.

3. You Carry the Ministry of Reconstruction

People may come to you shattered, but they will leave you strengthened because God works through you. A true trainer is not someone who imparts

information.
A true trainer is someone who imparts transformation.

VII. Every Believer Is a Builder in the Kingdom
Jesus was a carpenter not by accident. He came to rebuild human lives.
And He calls us to continue His work.
Brokenness → healing → maturity → ministry → multiplication.
This is the cycle of the kingdom.
You are not meant to remain a story of "*what God did for me.*" You are meant to carry the testimony of "*what God will now do through me.*"

- ✓ *A rebuilt person becomes a builder.*
- ✓ *A restored person becomes a restorer.*
- ✓ *A healed person becomes a healer.*
- ✓ *A lifted person lifts others.*

This is how revival spreads. This is how disciples are made. This is how families change. This is how communities transform. This is how the kingdom grows. One rebuilt life at a time.

VIII. Your Brokenness Is No Longer Your Identity — It Is Your Assignment

- ✓ *Your story is not a burden. It is a bridge.*
- ✓ *Your past is not a prison. It is a platform.*
- ✓ *Your pain is not wasted. It is woven into your ministry.*

God did not rebuild you so you could live quietly in the background. He rebuilt you so you could stand in the gap for those who are where you once were.
You are now a carrier of hope.
A voice of healing.
A vessel of grace.

A builder in the hands of God.

Your brokenness is no longer the chapter you avoid— it is the chapter someone else needs to survive their own journey.

You are not just healed. You are sent.

When the Master Finishes the Masterpiece: A Life That Reflects God's Glory

There is a holy moment in the life of every believer who has walked through brokenness—a moment when you pause, look back, and realize, "God really did it. He rebuilt me." What once felt like ruins have become pillars. What once were ashes have become beauty. What once were wounds have become wisdom. What once were tears have become testimonies.

This moment is not the end of your journey. It is the unveiling of the masterpiece the Master Artist has been working on all along.

God does not restore you halfway.

He does not leave you patched up with spiritual duct tape.

He completes what He starts.

The apostle Paul, who knew brokenness intimately, said: *"He who began a good work in you will be faithful to complete it."* — Philippians 1:6

God is not merely the Potter of your beginning— He is the Finisher of your becoming.

And when He finishes, His glory shines through you.

I. The Divine Completion: When God Says, "It Is Finished in You"

Every masterpiece has stages: shaping, breaking, refining, repairing, and polishing. Every believer experiences these same spiritual stages— but there comes a time when the repairing gives way to revealing.

A Kintsugi vessel is breathtaking not because it is perfect, but because it is whole.

Your life, once broken, is now held together by gold—the gold of God's mercy, grace, forgiveness, healing, and purpose.

Biblical Example: Joseph's Full-Circle Completion

When Joseph finally faced his brothers—the same brothers who betrayed him—he did not tremble, rage, or break again. Instead, he said: *"God has made me fruitful in the land of my suffering."* — Genesis 41:52

This is what completion looks like. He was no longer triggered by his past. He was no longer defined by his trauma. He was no longer shaped by bitterness. He stood as a masterpiece of God's glory— a man who could look at his darkest memories and say, *"God redeemed it all."*

This is where God wants to bring every believer.

II. A Life That Reflects His Glory: The Journey of Moses

Moses didn't shine with God's glory while he was a prince of Egypt.

He didn't shine while he was powerful.

He didn't shine while he had status.

He shone after he had been broken, humbled, emptied, and rebuilt.

"His face shone because he had been with the Lord." — Exodus 34:29

This is the life God finishes— a life that reflects Him so clearly that people notice without you saying a word.

Moses didn't try to shine. He simply reflected the One who rebuilt him. This is the destiny of every believer who walks through brokenness: Your life becomes a mirror for His glory.

III. The Evidence of a Finished Masterpiece: Transformation That Others Can See

A completed masterpiece is not a private trophy tucked away in God's workshop.
It is displayed for the world to see the glory of the Artist.

Biblical Example: The Gadarene Man

Once tormented, violent, broken beyond repair, he encountered Jesus and was restored—not partially, but fully.

Scripture says he was found: *"Sitting, clothed, and in his right mind."* — Mark 5:15

People who once feared him now marveled.

People who once avoided him now asked for his story.

His restoration became a public testimony of God's glory.

Jesus didn't just deliver him—

He commissioned him. *"Go and tell them what the Lord has done for you."* And he did.

And an entire region was impacted.

A finished masterpiece becomes a living sermon.

IV. Real-Life Story: Daniel, the Unexpected Pastor

Daniel once lived in deep depression. After losing his job and marriage in the same year, he spiraled into isolation. He felt worthless, convinced God had abandoned him. A small prayer group welcomed him, prayed with him weekly, reminded him of God's love, and slowly light returned to his eyes.

Today, Daniel leads the same prayer group that once carried him. People often say, *"There's a glow about him."* And it's true—his life carries a quiet authority, a compassion that feels like Christ's touch, a peace that disarms fear.

Daniel often says, *"I don't shine because I'm strong. I shine because God healed me."* His life reflects God's glory because the Master finished His work in him.

V. Real-Life Story: Mary Grace and the Children's Home

Mary Grace was abandoned as a child, growing up in orphanages and foster homes. Her scars ran deep. But when Christ found her in her twenties, He rebuilt her through years of inner healing, counseling, and discipleship.

In her forties, she opened a children's home for abandoned girls. When journalists once asked her, *"What inspired this work?"*

She smiled and said, *"I am simply giving away what God gave me—family."*

The brilliance of her life was not her ministry model but the God who finished healing her heart. Her life reflected glory because it reflected grace.

VI. The New Testament Pattern: Broken, Healed, Sent

Look at the apostles:

- ✓ *Peter—broken by denial, rebuilt by love.*
- ✓ *Paul—broken by blindness, rebuilt by revelation.*
- ✓ *John—broken by persecution, rebuilt by encounter.*
- ✓ *Mary Magdalene—broken by demons, rebuilt by devotion.*

- ✓ *Thomas—broken by doubt, rebuilt by evidence.*
- ✓ *The early church—broken by fear, rebuilt by fire.*

Every finished masterpiece in Scripture reflects the same truth: God does His best work through people who know they were once broken.

Because broken people never steal His glory— they reflect it.

VII. When Your Story Becomes His Story

A masterpiece is valuable not because of the clay, but because of the artist. When the

Master finishes His work in you, people no longer see your past—they see His power. They no longer see your scars—they see His grace. They no longer see your weakness—they see His strength. Your life becomes a canvas of Christ. This is not pride—it is purpose. It is not ego—it is evidence. It is not achievement—it is anointing.

VIII. The Marks of a Life Completed in God

A finished masterpiece is not flawless. It is surrendered.

You know God has completed a major work in you when:

- ✓ *You no longer fear your past.*
- ✓ *You no longer hide your scars.*
- ✓ *You no longer seek validation.*
- ✓ *You no longer walk in insecurity.*
- ✓ *You no longer depend on people to feel worthy.*
- ✓ *You no longer define yourself by what broke you.*

You walk in peace, purpose, humility, and quiet strength.
This is the fruit of divine completion.
You move from survivor → worshipper → witness → builder → reflection.
Your life becomes a window through which others see Christ.

IX. Glory Carriers: The Final Calling of the Restored Heart

God did not heal you to keep the healing quiet. He did not restore you to hide your restoration. He rebuilt you to radiate Him. You are a glory carrier.
Just like Moses, just like Joseph, just like Mary Magdalene, just like Peter, just like the early church— you reflect the glory of the One who finished His masterpiece.
And when heaven looks at you, heaven sees beauty. Heaven sees purpose. Heaven sees destiny. Heaven sees reflection. Heaven sees a vessel that was once shattered, now shining with gold, held together by grace, and revealing the craftsmanship of God.
You are a masterpiece, not because you are perfect, but because you are His.

Living Restored: The Daily Practices of a Rebuilt Life

Restoration is not a one-time event. It is a way of living. Many people experience an initial breakthrough, a powerful encounter, a moment of healing—but they do not know how to *stay* healed, how to *walk* in that wholeness every day, how to protect what God rebuilt inside them.

In Scripture, every person God restored learned to walk in a new rhythm—a daily lifestyle that protected the grace they had received.

- ✓ *David learned it in the wilderness*
- ✓ *Joseph learned it in prison*
- ✓ *Daniel learned it in Babylon*
- ✓ *Peter learned it after the resurrection*
- ✓ *Mary Magdalene learned it at Jesus' feet*
- ✓ *Paul learned it through daily surrender*
- ✓ *And millions have learned it since.*

A rebuilt life must be *lived* intentionally.

Restoration is a gift—but remaining restored is a habit. Just as a Kintsugi bowl must be handled carefully to preserve its beauty, a restored life must be lived with spiritual and emotional disciplines that keep the cracks filled with gold.

This chapter explores those daily practices—simple, practical, Spirit-breathed rhythms that help a restored believer remain strong, steady, joyful, and fruitful.

I. Spiritual Habits: Daily Anchors for a Rebuilt Soul

A restored life must have restored roots. Without spiritual rhythms, old wounds quickly reopen and old patterns slowly return.

The Habit of Returning to God Daily

David prayed, *"Restore to me the joy of Your salvation and renew a right spirit within me."* — Psalm 51:12

David had learned that restoration was not a moment, but a maintenance. He did not rely on yesterday's encounter. He sought fresh grace every morning.

Quiet Time: Your Daily Kintsugi Moment

Every day you sit with Jesus, something sacred happens.

- ✓ *Your cracks are refilled with gold.*
- ✓ *Your mind is renewed.*
- ✓ *Your heart is strengthened.*
- ✓ *Your spirit is re-centered.*

This is not religious duty. It is relational oxygen.

Scripture Example: Mary at Jesus' Feet

While Martha was busy, Mary sat at His feet, absorbing every word. Jesus said: *"Mary has chosen the better part."* — Luke 10:42

The restored life chooses presence over performance.

Prayer: The Heart's Daily Reset

Prayer is not only words—it is alignment. It is the moment you allow God to reorder your thoughts, desires, and decisions.

Real-Life Story: Jacob's New Rhythm

Jacob (not the patriarch) had lived most of his life reacting—anger, anxiety, compulsive habits. After his restoration process, he learned to pray every morning before checking his phone or stepping into work.

He later said, *"That fifteen minutes keeps me sane. It keeps me whole."*

His restored life depended on a restored rhythm.

II. Emotional Hygiene: Protecting the Heart God Healed

The heart is the most delicate part of your restoration. Just as you wash your hands daily, the soul must be cleaned of invisible dirt—fear, resentment, negative thinking, shame, and spiritual fatigue.

Biblical Blueprints for Emotional Health

David practiced emotional hygiene when he wrote the Psalms. He poured out his frustrations, tears, doubts, and anger before God instead of burying them.

Elijah practiced emotional hygiene when he allowed God to confront his exhaustion, fear, and loneliness under the broom tree (1 Kings 19). God did not scold him—He replenished him.

Paul practiced emotional hygiene when he taught believers to *"take every thought captive"* (2 Corinthians 10:5).

Daily Emotional Check-ins

A restored believer learns to ask:

- ✓ *"Why am I feeling this way?"*
- ✓ *"What is the lie I'm believing?"*
- ✓ *"Where did I give room to fear today?"*
- ✓ *"Is my heart carrying offense, sadness, or heaviness?"*

Real-Life Story: Nisha's Evening Ritual

Nisha suffered years of emotional abuse, and though God healed her deeply, she realized old anxieties resurfaced whenever she didn't watch her inner world.

So every night she spent ten minutes journaling:

"What did I feel today? Why? What did God say about it?"

This small practice protected her restoration more than anything else.

III. Community & Accountability: The Circle That Keeps You Standing

No one stays restored alone. Scripture is unambiguous about this.

- ✓ *Paul had Barnabas.*
- ✓ *Moses had Aaron.*
- ✓ *Ruth had Naomi.*
- ✓ *David had Jonathan.*
- ✓ *The disciples had each other.*
- ✓ *Even Jesus had Peter, James, and John.*

The restored life requires spiritual community.

Biblical Foundation: Ecclesiastes 4:9–10: *"Two are better than one… if one falls, the other helps him up."*

When you walk with others, you grow. When you isolate yourself, you regress.

The Power of Honest Community

Accountability is not about control—it is about covering. It is someone asking:

- ✓ *"How is your heart?"*
- ✓ *"Are you walking in temptation?"*
- ✓ *"Are you staying rooted in the Word?"*
- ✓ *"Are you carrying an offense?"*

And answering not from fear, but from trust.

Real-Life Story: The "Three Brothers" Group

Three men—*Joel*, *Prakash*, and *Eden*—had each overcome deep addictions. They met weekly for prayer, confession, encouragement, and Scripture.

They often said: *"Our strength is shared."*

Years later, all three are leaders—teaching, mentoring, and counseling, not because they are perfect, but because they learned to remain connected.

If the enemy can isolate you, he can influence you. If community surrounds you, the enemy loses his reach.

IV. Purpose-Driven Living: The Fuel of a Rebuilt Life

A restored believer must have direction. Purpose is the foundation under your feet. It is the thing that makes you get up in the morning with conviction.

Biblical Example: Peter After Restoration

After denying Jesus, Peter could have lived in guilt forever. But Jesus restored him and then immediately gave him purpose: *"Feed My sheep."* — John 21:17

Jesus did not merely heal Peter— He re-commissioned him. Purpose protects restoration.

Biblical Example: Paul's Driving Purpose

Paul, once a persecutor, became unstoppable because he lived with a single focus:

"This one thing I do…" — Philippians 3:13

Purpose narrowed his heart, purified his motives, and strengthened his spirit.

Real-Life Story: Maria's Mission

Maria had struggled with depression for years. After healing, she felt God stirring her to volunteer at a local shelter. She didn't feel eloquent or *"qualified,"* but she had compassion.

One day she told me, *"Serving others keeps me healed. It reminds me I'm part of something bigger."* Purpose turned her restoration into fuel for others.

Purpose Creates Stability

When you live for something larger than your pain:

- ✓ *You stop overthinking*
- ✓ *You stop reliving old wounds*

- ✓ *You stop spiraling inward*
- ✓ *You stop fearing the future*
- ✓ *You stop shrinking back into insecurity*

Purpose stabilizes the soul.
Purpose matures the heart.
Purpose keeps you aligned with heaven.

V. The Daily Rhythm of a Rebuilt Life

A restored life is not dramatic. It is consistent. Steady. Rhythmic. Faithful.

The man who prays daily doesn't need a crisis to find God.

The woman who guards her heart doesn't break easily under pressure.

The believer who walks in community doesn't fall silently in the night.

The disciple who lives on purpose doesn't drift into confusion.

Restoration is maintained in daily decisions.
Not big ones—small ones.
Not occasional ones—ongoing ones.

Every day you practice these rhythms, you remain a Kintsugi masterpiece— cracks filled with fresh grace, heart anchored in truth, life built on stability.

VI. The Restored Life Becomes a Restoring Life

When you live restored daily, something supernatural happens:

- ✓ Your life becomes a source of healing for others without you even trying.
- ✓ People feel safe around you.
- ✓ People sense peace from you.
- ✓ People receive wisdom through you.
- ✓ People see Jesus in you.
- ✓ Your lifestyle becomes your ministry.

- ✓ Your habits become your testimony.
- ✓ Your consistency becomes your witness.
- ✓ Your joy becomes your invitation.

A restored life is a lighthouse, guiding others through storms you once survived.

VII. God Doesn't Just Heal You — He Teaches You How to Stay Whole

A rebuilt life requires daily maintenance—not out of fear, but out of love. Not out of insecurity, but out of maturity. Not because you're fragile, but because you're valuable. The more beautiful the Kintsugi piece, the more intentionally it must be handled.

You are precious to God.

Your healing matters.

Your heart matters.

Your calling matters.

This is not about discipline alone— it is about devotion. Not about strictness— but about stewardship. Not about rules— but about relationship.

Living restored is living close to Jesus.

When the Child Who Troubles You Is the Child God Has Called

Every parent dreams of seeing their children walk in wisdom, discipline, and purpose. But not every child takes a straight path. Some take the longer, harder, messier road—one filled with confusion, rebellion, wrong friendships, and decisions that make parents cry privately and shout helplessly. And yet, these very children are often the ones heaven has marked long before anyone else can see it.

I know this, because I lived it.

For years, my son gave us more trouble than we ever expected. School became a battleground. Teachers' complaints were endless—poor grades, bunking classes, troubling others, falling into the wrong crowd, and showing a surprising creativity… in mischief. At home, he pushed boundaries, tested patience, and seemed determined to explore every wrong turn. I still remember the day he took my car—without permission—while I was away. He returned it with dents and scratches I didn't even know were possible. My wife June would be on her knees everyday, praying for him and his safety. Those were the days we wondered, *"Lord, where is this boy heading?"*

But what we saw as trouble, God saw as potential. What we saw as rebellion, God saw as raw material. What we saw as a wandering spirit, God saw as someone who would one day lead others home.

We did not recognize the calling. But God did. And He used the right man to draw it out.

It was nearly five years ago, during a Watch Night service, that Prophet Jerome Fernando—whom God used mightily to see beyond the surface—called my son out. In front of everyone, he identified what heaven had already written:

There was a calling on this young man's life.

In that moment, everything made sense—the restlessness, the struggle, the instability, the searching heart. God had been shaping him, even in his rebellion. God had been preparing him, even in his mistakes. God had been forming a pastor in places we thought were failures.

Today, that same son stands as a fulfillment of prophecy.

Today, that same son—once the cause of endless frustration—is leading a full-fledged church in Chennai: (The Chennai Chapter of The Glorious Church- founded by Prophet Jerome Fernando).

When I watch him preach, lead, and minister, I often think back to the boy who dented my car and troubled his teachers. And I realize:

- ✓ *A troubled child is not a hopeless child.*
- ✓ *A rebellious child is not a rejected child.*
- ✓ *A complicated child may very well be a called child.*

The Bible is filled with such stories.

Jacob deceived. Joseph's brothers rebelled. Moses ran. David strayed. Peter denied. Paul persecuted. Yet all of them were called. All of them were chosen. All of them were used—not because they were qualified, but because they were available to God when the moment came.

God has a strange, beautiful habit of choosing the unlikely.

So, if you are a parent reading this, let this chapter speak hope into your heart: The child who gives you the most trouble may be the child with the greatest calling.

The one who frustrates you today may be the one who will minister tomorrow. The one who tests your patience may one day teach others how to follow God.

Don't lose hope. Don't give up. Don't label your child by their mistakes. Because God never calls the qualified—He qualifies the called.

And sometimes all it takes is the right voice, the right moment, the right man of God, to call out what heaven has hidden inside a wandering child.

We thank God for this mighty Man of God, Prophet Jerome Fernando—because through him, God unlocked a destiny we were blind to. Without that prophetic word, we may never have recognized the treasure buried beneath the trouble.

Parents, hear this:

You don't need a perfect child. You need a praying heart. And the right prophetic atmosphere.

Because one divine encounter can rewrite your child's entire future.

So as you continue reading this book, or as you sit before God in prayer, remember:

- ✓ *God can use anyone.*
- ✓ *God can call anyone.*
- ✓ *God can anoint anyone.*
- ✓ *And especially the ones who seem the least likely.*

Your child may look broken now. But in God's hands, they are being built. This chapter is a witness of that truth.

Diagnostic Tools for Counselors & Pastors

Every counselor, pastor, and spiritual mentor knows that healing rarely begins with answers—it begins with the right questions. Ministry to the broken is not about offering solutions quickly; it is about discerning the deeper reality beneath a person's pain. Sometimes the wound they speak aloud is not the wound that needs healing. Sometimes the story they present is the surface layer covering a deeper rupture buried under years of silence. As Jesus so beautifully demonstrated, the greatest healers listen more than they speak.

In Scripture, God Himself uses diagnostic questions long before He provides direction. When Adam hides in shame, God does not immediately restore him. He first asks, *"Where are you?"* (Genesis 3:9). Not because God lacked information, but because Adam needed awareness. When Elijah is depressed under the broom tree, God asks him, *"What are you doing here?"* (1 Kings 19:9). When Hagar flees in despair, the angel asks, *"Where have you come from, and where are you going?"* (Genesis 16:8).

These divine questions expose heart conditions, uncover fears, reveal lies, and bring clarity to confusion. A counselor's greatest skill, therefore, is holy curiosity—a gentle capacity to draw out the truth a person has forgotten, ignored, or never dared to say.

Healing begins where understanding begins.

I. Asking the Right Questions — The Ministry of Holy Curiosity

A counselor is not a detective searching for guilt, but a shepherd searching for the injured lamb. Questions, when asked with compassion, open doors within the heart that pain has locked. The right question can soften anger, unravel denial, calm fear, and help the broken articulate what they have carried silently for years.

Jesus was the master of diagnostic questions. When a blind man came to Him, the answer seemed obvious—yet Jesus still asked, "*What do you want Me to do for you?*" (Mark 10:51). He knew that unspoken desires hinder healing. When the lame man at Bethesda had been lying there for thirty-eight years, Jesus did not simply command him to stand. He asked, *"Do you want to be healed?"* (John 5:6). Counselors today often discover that people are attached to their pain more than they admit. Jesus' question pierced that bond.

I once counseled *Leela*, a woman convinced her depression was caused by her husband's neglect. For months, she angrily blamed him. But one day I asked, *"Leela, if your husband suddenly became the man you want, what would you feel?"* She stared blankly, then whispered, *"I don't know what I would become without this pain."* That question revealed she feared healing more than brokenness—because brokenness was familiar.

Diagnostic questions bring revelation.
Revelation creates movement.
Movement opens doors to healing.

II. Identifying the Root Issues — Healing Beneath the Symptoms

Many people come to counseling with surface-level complaints: *"I feel anxious," "I get angry too quickly,"*

"My husband doesn't understand me," "I can't stop falling back into addiction." But these are symptoms. True ministry digs deeper.

Just as a doctor examines the body to locate infection, a counselor examines the heart to find the root. Emotional infections—bitterness, abandonment, rejection, guilt, shame, trauma, fear—always produce symptoms. A person struggling with rage is often a person with buried sorrow. A person terrified of conflict often has a wound of past rejection. A person clinging to destructive relationships is often carrying childhood insecurity.

Biblical Pattern: Jesus and the Samaritan Woman

When the Samaritan woman spoke about water, Jesus addressed her marriages. When she spoke about religion, He addressed her wounds.

When she hid her shame, He uncovered her identity.

Jesus always reached the root because He knew surface fixes cannot heal deep fractures.

Example: "Ajay's Anger"

Ajay sought help because he had uncontrollable anger. He blamed his temper on stress and work pressure. But as we talked, a deeper wound emerged—he had grown up with a father who criticized everything he did. His rage, we discovered, was really unprocessed grief. He had never mourned his childhood. The moment that root surfaced, healing finally began.

Example: "Meera's Fear of Abandonment"

Meera felt panicked whenever her husband traveled for work. On the surface, it looked like insecurity in marriage. But through prayer and conversation, she confessed a childhood memory—her mother leaving her at a train station by mistake when she was six.

That trauma shaped her adult fears. Addressing the root dissolved the symptoms.

A wise counselor listens not only to what is said, but also to what is not said. Beneath every story lies a wound waiting to be named.

III. Mapping Emotional Wounds — Understanding the Landscape of Pain

Mapping emotional wounds is not about labeling people; it is about understanding them. Every wounded person carries an internal map—fault lines where their soul cracked, territories where they avoid going, and regions where pain still breathes.

The Psalmist understood this when he wrote, *"You have searched me, Lord, and You know me… You perceive my thoughts from afar."* — Psalm 139:1–2

God knows every emotional bruise, every unspoken fear, every hidden memory. Pastors and counselors must learn to see a person the way God sees them—not only for who they are, but for what shaped them.

Wound Mapping Through Storytelling

Most emotional wounds reveal themselves through stories. When people talk about their past, they leave clues. When they describe their relationships, habits, fears, dreams, or failures, the heart speaks through fragments.

One of the most effective ways to map wounds is simply to let people narrate their life without interruption. Stories create pathways into hidden chambers.

Biblical Example: Elijah's Breakdown

When Elijah collapsed under the broom tree, God allowed him to express his fear, exhaustion, and

despair. Elijah said, *"I am no better than my ancestors."*
He revealed his wound—an identity shaped by comparison and failure.
God then ministered to the deeper wound: exhaustion, loneliness, fear, and misplaced expectations.

Real-Life Example: "Anand's Perfectionism"

Anand looked successful—stable job, polite manner, disciplined habits. But he was brittle inside. His perfectionism was not ambition; it was fear. As we mapped his story, he shared how his mother used to punish him for scoring anything less than 95%. Every mistake as a child felt like rejection. His wound was not perfectionism—it was conditional love.
The moment his wound was identified, the shackles of performance loosened.

IV. The Counselor's Role — A Guide, Not a Surgeon

A counselor is not the hero of the story. The Holy Spirit is. A counselor does not "fix" wounds. They reveal them, expose the lies beneath them, and guide the broken to the One who heals.
Healing belongs to Jesus.
Understanding belongs to us.
Jesus Himself said the Spirit would *"search all things"* (1 Corinthians 2:10). Counselors simply partner with that searching.

The Counselor as a Safe Place

Most broken people do not need answers first. They need safety. They need someone who will not judge tears, rush their story, or recoil at their scars.
When a person feels safe, they share honestly.

When they share honestly, wounds come into the light.
When wounds come into the light, God begins His work.

V. The Goal: Seeing What God Sees

Every counselor's ultimate diagnostic tool is this prayer: *"Lord, show me what You see."*
God sees the child behind the addict, the ache behind the anger, the sorrow behind the sin, the fear behind the failure, the longing behind the loneliness.
When we see what God sees, we minister to people's hearts, not their behavior. We treat causes, not symptoms. We heal wounds, not reputations.
This is the sacred calling of every counselor, pastor, and shepherd— to look at a person and see both the wound and the masterpiece, both the broken place and the gold God wants to fill it with.
The diagnostic tools in your hands are not academic—they are spiritual. Questions become instruments of insight. Attentive listening becomes a pathway to revelation. Discernment becomes a lamp guiding you to the hidden fractures within the soul. And once the wound is found, healing can finally begin.

Healing Exercises, Prayers, and Practices

One of the most beautiful truths about God is that He is not only a Restorer in theory—He is a Restorer in practice. Healing in the Kingdom is not accidental; it happens intentionally, slowly, gently, and deeply through repeated encounters with the Healer Himself. As the Great Physician of the soul, God invites us into rhythms, practices, and spiritual exercises that strengthen our spirit, renew our minds, and align our hearts with His truth.

Many people wrongly assume that healing is something God does *to* a person. But often, healing is something God does *with* a person. Restoration is a partnership—God brings the power, and we bring the posture. God provides the grace, and we provide the surrender. God supplies the truth, and we open the wound.

This chapter provides simple, biblical, Christ-centered exercises that individuals, counselors, pastors, families, and small groups can use. These practices are born from Scripture, tested in real pastoral settings, and rooted in the Holy Spirit's gentle work.

I. Healing Through Prayer — Entering the Presence of the Healer

Prayer is not merely the act of speaking to God; it is stepping into the emotional operating room of His love. People often come to God like the woman with the issue of blood—trembling, unclean, desperate, and uncertain. Yet it is in prayer that their trembling becomes trust and their desperation becomes healing.

One of the most effective prayer patterns for the broken is what I call "**The Four Movements of Healing Prayer**": Come. Confess. Cry. Commune. Not as formula, but as a rhythm.

To illustrate, let me share about *Ruth*, a woman who carried unresolved grief from a miscarriage she never spoke about. In counseling, she refused to cry, insisting she was "strong in faith." But one day, she finally prayed honestly, *"Lord, I'm scared to bring this to You because it feels too heavy."* She didn't quote a single verse that day. She just cried. And in that moment, healing began—not because she said the right words, but because she brought the real wound into God's presence.

Another example is *Savio*, a pastor so burnt out that he prayed only out of duty. His healing began when he whispered, *"God, I don't know how to pray anymore, but I don't want to pretend."* That raw confession opened the door to restoration.

True healing prayer is simply this: Your real heart in God's real presence.

II. Scripture Declarations — Rewiring the Mind With God's Truth

The enemy attacks the mind because he knows the mind shapes identity. This is why Paul wrote, *"Be transformed by the renewing of your mind"* (Romans 12:2). Truth spoken repeatedly becomes truth believed. And truth believed becomes truth lived.

Declarations are not magic words; they are biblical truths spoken into places where lies have lived for too long.

When a person makes Scripture declarations, their spirit stands up straighter. Their thinking shifts. Their internal dialogue changes. The lies that controlled them begin to crumble under the weight of God's voice.

I remember *Daniel*, a young man trapped in shame after a moral failure. His mind tormented him with one sentence: *"You're beyond repair."* I asked him to declare Romans 8:1 every morning for thirty days: *"There is therefore now no condemnation for those who are in Christ Jesus."*

He told me, *"At first I didn't believe it. But after a few days, the verse stopped sounding like a verse and began sounding like God."*

Likewise, *Esther*, a widow, battled fear every night. She began declaring Isaiah 41:10 before sleep: *"Fear not, for I am with you."*

Her fear didn't disappear instantly, but her courage grew daily because truth the enemy had been hiding became truth she now held.

Declarations reposition the soul.

Here are a few examples you can offer those who counsel:

"God is near to the brokenhearted" (Psalm 34:18).

"I am God's workmanship, not my wounds' product" (Ephesians 2:10).

"His strength is made perfect in my weakness" (2 Corinthians 12:9).

"All things are being worked for my good" (Romans 8:28).

"He restores my soul" (Psalm 23:3).

When these truths become a person's daily language, their healing accelerates.

III. Inner Healing Practices — Welcoming the Holy Spirit Into the Broken Places

Inner healing is not psychology and it is not mysticism. It is the Holy Spirit touching areas of the heart that human hands cannot reach. No yoga, no rituals, no mantras. Only Jesus, Scripture, prayer, and the Spirit.

The simplest and most biblically sound inner healing practices are the ones Jesus Himself used with hurting people.

1. The "Jesus, Where Were You?" Encounter

This exercise helps people revisit painful memories with Jesus instead of revisiting them alone.

A young man named *Rahul* always felt abandoned by his father, who left when he was nine. During a session, I asked Rahul to close his eyes and think about the moment he watched his father pack his bags and leave. Then I gently asked, *"Rahul, where was Jesus in that moment?"*

At first there was silence. Then tears. Then he whispered, *"He was sitting beside the boy I was… crying with me."*

That moment didn't erase years of pain, but it healed the root of identity: He was never alone. This practice echoes Isaiah 43:2— *"When you pass through the waters, I will be with you."*

2. The "Letting Go With Open Hands" Prayer

Many people hold wounds tightly because they fear what will happen if they let go. This practice helps them release pain physically and spiritually.

A widow named *Mary*, who lost her husband to cancer, struggled to let go of the bitterness she held against God. One day, I asked her to place her

palms upward and imagine placing her grief into Jesus' hands.
She began to sob and whispered, *"Lord, I give You this anger. It's too heavy to hold."*
In that simple act of physical surrender, emotional surrender followed.
Jesus said, *"Come to Me, all who are weary and burdened..."* (Matthew 11:28). Letting go creates space for rest.

3. The "Blessing the Wound" Exercise
This is not thanking God *for* the pain, but thanking Him for His presence *in* the pain.
A woman named *Kavitha* felt deep shame from years of verbal abuse. One day we prayed, "*Lord, thank You that this wound is not the end of my story. Thank You that You will use this place to show Your glory."*
As she prayed this, hope began to rise—not for what happened, but for what God could build through it.
Joseph did this when he declared, *"God meant it for good"* (Genesis 50:20).
He blessed the wound, not because it was good, but because God was greater.

IV. A Life of Ongoing Healing — Walking Daily With the Master Restorer
Healing is not a one-time event. It is a journey with the Savior. A broken person may feel healed today and wounded again tomorrow. But that does not mean they are failing. It means they are human.
God heals layer by layer, season by season, memory by memory.
The daily practices in this chapter—honest prayer, scripture declarations, inner healing exercises—become the ongoing companionship of the restored

believer. They teach hearts to breathe again, thoughts to align again, and spirits to rise again.

A restored life is not a life without battles. It is a life where Jesus enters the battles with you.

50 Scriptures on Brokenness & Restoration

Below is a curated list of 50 powerful Scriptures on Brokenness and Restoration, covering emotional healing, spiritual renewal, God's nearness, rebuilding, deliverance, and divine purpose.

All references are from the Bible, arranged to help pastors, counselors, teachers, and individuals in their healing journeys.

These verses can be used for:

- ✓ Sermons
- ✓ Counseling sessions
- ✓ Personal prayer
- ✓ Journaling
- ✓ Scripture declarations
- ✓ Healing workshops

Every verse is directly related to brokenness, healing, restoration, rebuilding, renewal, comfort, and God's redemptive work.

1. Psalm 147:3
"He heals the brokenhearted and binds up their wounds."
2. Isaiah 57:15
"I dwell… with the one who is contrite and lowly in spirit, to revive the spirit of the lowly."
3. Psalm 34:18
"The Lord is close to the brokenhearted and saves those crushed in spirit."
4. Psalm 51:17
"A broken and contrite heart, O God, You will not despise."
5. Isaiah 61:1

"He has sent Me to bind up the brokenhearted… to proclaim freedom for the captives."

6. Joel 2:25

"I will restore to you the years that the locust has eaten."

7. Jeremiah 30:17

"For I will restore health to you, and your wounds I will heal."

8. Isaiah 43:2

"When you pass through the waters, I will be with you."

9. Romans 8:28

"In all things God works for the good of those who love Him."

10. Psalm 23:3

"He restores my soul."

11. 1 Peter 5:10

"The God of all grace… will Himself restore, confirm, strengthen and establish you."

12. 2 Corinthians 12:9

"My grace is sufficient for you, for My power is made perfect in weakness."

13. Matthew 11:28

"Come to Me, all who are weary and burdened, and I will give you rest."

14. Isaiah 40:29

"He gives strength to the weary and increases the power of the weak."

15. Hosea 6:1

"He has torn us, but He will heal us; He has injured us, but He will bind up our wounds."

16. Psalm 147:3

"He binds up their wounds."

17. Lamentations 3:22–23

"His mercies never fail… they are new every morning."

18. Micah 7:8

"Though I fall, I will rise; though I sit in darkness, the Lord will be my light."

19. Psalm 73:26

"My flesh and my heart may fail, but God is the strength of my heart."

20. Proverbs 24:16

"The righteous fall seven times and rise again."

21. Psalm 30:5

"Weeping may stay for the night, but joy comes in the morning."

22. Jeremiah 29:11

"I know the plans I have for you… plans to prosper you, not to harm you."

23. Isaiah 42:3

"A bruised reed He will not break, and a smoldering wick He will not snuff out."

24. Psalm 130:7

"With the Lord there is steadfast love, and with Him is plentiful redemption."

25. Zechariah 9:12

"Return to your stronghold, O prisoners of hope; today I declare I will restore double to you."

26. Ezekiel 36:26

"I will give you a new heart and put a new spirit in you."

27. Psalm 145:14

"The Lord upholds all who fall and lifts up all who are bowed down."

28. Isaiah 49:16

"I have engraved you on the palms of My hands."

29. Matthew 5:4

"Blessed are those who mourn, for they will be comforted."

30. John 14:27

"My peace I give you… do not let your hearts be troubled."

31. Psalm 55:22

"Cast your cares on the Lord and He will sustain you."

32. Philippians 1:6

"He who began a good work in you will be faithful to complete it."

33. 2 Corinthians 5:17

"If anyone is in Christ, he is a new creation."

34. Revelation 21:5

"Behold, I make all things new."

35. James 5:15

"The prayer of faith will save the sick, and the Lord will raise him up."

36. Psalm 46:1

"God is our refuge and strength, an ever-present help in trouble."

37. Nahum 1:7

"The Lord is good, a stronghold in the day of trouble."

38. Psalm 91:15

"I will be with him in trouble; I will deliver him and honor him."

39. Hebrews 4:16

"Let us approach God's throne of grace… to find mercy and help."

40. John 16:33

"In this world you will have trouble. But take heart! I have overcome the world."

41. Psalm 32:7

"You are my hiding place; You preserve me from trouble."

42. Isaiah 58:12
"You will rebuild the ancient ruins… you will be called Repairer of the Breach."
43. Psalm 40:2
"He lifted me out of the pit, out of the mud and mire."
44. Genesis 50:20
"You meant evil against me, but God meant it for good."
45. Luke 4:18
"He has sent Me to proclaim freedom… and set the oppressed free."
46. Psalm 18:28
"You, Lord, keep my lamp burning; my God turns my darkness into light."
47. Isaiah 55:12
"You will go out with joy and be led forth with peace."
48. Zephaniah 3:17
"He will rejoice over you with singing."
49. Hebrews 12:13
"Make straight paths for your feet, so that the lame may not be disabled, but rather healed."
50. Psalm 126:5–6
"Those who sow in tears will reap with songs of joy."

Epilogue
Better than New

There comes a moment in every restoration story when you pause, look back, and realize that the path you thought would destroy you actually brought you to the feet of the One who rebuilt you. As I finish writing these final pages, I find myself reflecting on the refrigerators repaired, the burnt guitars resurrected, the slum families transformed, and the hidden wounds God patiently stitched together in people I have loved and prayed for.

What I have discovered over the years is profoundly simple yet deeply divine:

God does not restore us to what we were. He restores us into what we were always meant to be. He makes us better than new.

A guitar that once lay in eight charred pieces now sings with a clarity it never carried before. A marriage once cold as winter now reflects warmth that wasn't present in its early years. A grieving widow who could barely breathe now comforts others with an authority only suffering can teach. A former addict now leads young men into freedom with a passion deeper than any sermon I could preach.

This is the miracle of biblical restoration. God never returns things to their original condition. He transforms them into an entirely new creation.

A God Who Writes Better Endings

The Old Testament closes with a broken nation, a wounded people, and a longing that seems unanswered. Yet the New Testament opens with Emmanuel—God with us stepping into the story

Himself. God never leaves His people with unfinished wounds.

Joseph's brothers meant evil. God meant good. And the good was better than the life Joseph once dreamed of.

Job lost everything. God restored him. And the restoration was not a replacement—it was a revelation. He once knew God by hearing; he ended knowing Him by seeing.

Peter denied Jesus with curses. But Jesus restored him with a calling. And the man who once crumbled under the voice of a servant girl later thundered the Gospel before thousands.

Everywhere you look in Scripture, God takes shattered people and makes them into masterpieces. Not recycled. Not refurbished. Reborn.

You Are Not the Person Who Entered This Book

Somewhere between these pages, God touched something in you.

Maybe He exposed a wound you didn't know was still alive.

Maybe He healed one you thought would never close.

Maybe He whispered words that rewrote years of lies.

Maybe He reminded you that your life still matters, that your story still has purpose, that your future still carries promise.

Like *Maria*, who spent years believing abuse had scarred her beyond repair until God slowly rebuilt her into a counselor who now heals others. Her tears became tools. Her story became strength.

Or *Daniel*, once suicidal, now leading prayer meetings where others rediscover hope. He often says, *"God didn't just save my life—He rewrote it."*
Or *Jacob*, a man who grew up fatherless and bitter, but after encountering God's healing, became a father to children without fathers. He became what he never had.
You, too, are on the edge of a new identity.
You have been broken, yes. But you have also been rebuilt. And rebuilt things carry glory that untouched things never know.

A Final Encouragement: Walk Forward Without Fear
You do not have to fear your past anymore.
You do not have to fear your future anymore.
You do not have to fear your weaknesses anymore.
You do not have to fear whether God is disappointed in you.
You are His.
You always have been.
You always will be.
The hands that shaped Adam from dust are the same hands shaping you now. The voice that called Lazarus out of the tomb is the same voice calling you into new life. The heart that embraced the prodigal is the same heart beating over your restoration story.
You are not walking away from this book alone.
You are walking forward with the One who promised: *"I will never leave you nor forsake you."*
Your brokenness has not disqualified you. It has positioned you. It has deepened you. It has awakened you. It has prepared you.
You are not just surviving. You are rising. You are becoming.

You are standing as living proof that God still rebuilds, still restores, still resurrects.
And now, as you step into your next chapter, may you carry this truth with you:
The cracks you carry are not evidence of failure. They are evidence of glory.

Identity Declaration for the Reader

(To be spoken aloud, slowly, prayerfully, as a final sealing of truth)

"I am loved by God deeply, eternally, and unconditionally.
My brokenness is not my identity; it is the place where God met me.
I am not defined by what hurt me—I am defined by the One who healed me.
God restores my soul, renews my strength, and rebuilds my life.
What was lost will be returned.
What was damaged will be healed.
What was shattered will be made beautiful.
I am a masterpiece in the hands of the Master.
I am forgiven.
I am chosen.
I am whole.
I am new.
And from this day forward, I will walk in purpose, hope, and divine courage.
I am broken no longer.
I am rebuilt in Christ.
I am better than new."

About the Author
'GERARD ASSEY'

Gerard Assey is a Graduate in Economics, a PGD in Management (HRD) and holds a Doctorate in Leadership. Gerard holds several International Qualifications in Sales, Debt Collection, Training & Teaching, and is a 'Fellow' of the prestigious 'Institute of Sales & Marketing Management'-UK, a Certified NLP Practitioner, a 'Certified Trainer', an 'Accredited Management Teacher-Behavioral Sciences', a 'Certified Competency Facilitator', a 'Certified Management Consultant'- (the International credentials of a professional management consultant, awarded in accordance with global standards of the ICMCI); and a Certification from the University of Michigan in 'Successful Negotiation: Essential Strategies and Skills'

He is also a Member of the 'National Association of Sales Professionals' backed with several years experience in varied industries, both in India and Overseas. He also holds an 'Etiquette Consultant' Certification from the USA (by Sue Fox, Author of Best Seller: 'Business Etiquette for Dummies'. She has trained some of the top celebrities' world over). He was also a recipient of a scholarship for extensive training in Japan on 'Corporate Management for India'.

Gerard Assey is 'Founder & Chief Corporate Trainer' of the Group: '**Citius, Altius, Fortius Unlimited**'- an organization that **celebrated 20 years of Glorious Service** in 2021, focusing on 3 Core Competencies:

People. Performance. Profit; in functional areas of Sales & Marketing, HR & Organizational Development, covering Recruitment, Training & Consultancy!

Having managed organizations with large Sales Forces in India & Overseas, his specialization cover extensive areas of Sales Training (All levels - Presentation, Negotiation, Key/ Strategic Accounts Management & Managerial Skills for all sectors), Bid Proposal/ Capture Planning/ Management Trainings, Retail Sales, Customer Service & Customer Retention Programs, Training for Prevention & Collection of Debt, Self & Personal Development Programs (Time Management, Teamwork & Team Building, Business Etiquette & Personal Grooming, Leadership & Managerial Skills, People Management Skills, Train-the-Trainer etc), including preparation of Custom-designed Business Manuals for Internal (HR, Induction, and Sales etc) & External use (Instruction, User Manuals).

Gerard has successfully conducted over 6490 Trainings & Workshops (as of Nov '25) all across India, Middle East, Africa, Europe & S.E. Asia. Besides public programs conducted regularly, both in India & Overseas, he has some of the top names as clients whom he services from Single Owners to large Public & Government undertakings, covering all sectors, for their in-house needs.

His website: www.CollectionSkills.com is the only one in this part of the world to be featured in the 'Collections & Credit Risk Magazine-USA' under 'Who's Who in Training' and ranks TOP, along with other websites listed below on most search engines.

Gerard is author of 210 Books already (Dec 2025), all the books being available on all online platforms and outlets as E-books and Paperbacks

A few of our business related books:

1. Bite-sized Bits on Commonsense Management
2. Heart to Heart on Life's Principles'
3. How to become a Successful Manager
4. The Sales Professionals' Master Workbook of S.Y.S.T.E.M.S
5. The Professional Business Email Etiquette Handbook & Guide
6. The Professional Business Video-Conferencing Etiquette Handbook & Guide
7. Professional Presentation Skills
8. Exceptional Customer Service
9. Professional Tele-Marketing Skills
10. Professional Debt Collection Skills
11. The G.R.E.A.T. Sales & Service Workbook
12. Sales Training Advantage for Results (*The Ultimate Sales Training Manual to enable you stand out as a S.T.A.R.*)
13. CEO Daily Planner & Organizer
14. The Sales Professionals' Master Daily Planner
15. The Professional Debt Collector's Master Daily Planner
16. My Daily Planner & Organizer
17. MY EMERGENCY INFORMATION RECORD (Family Emergency & Peace of Mind Planner)
18. The Ultimate Therapist & Counselors Planner and Organizer
19. Building an Ethical Workplace
20. Managing Relationships at Work
21. Managing Business Meetings Effectively
22. Effective Delegation Skills
23. Goal Setting for Success
24. B2B Selling by Email
25. Professional Business Etiquette & Grooming
26. Dining Etiquette & Table Manners
27. Effective Networking Skills
28. Grooming, Etiquette & Manners for Teens, Young Adults & Future Leaders
29. Inter-Personal Skills
30. Get Ready, Get Hired!
31. Selling in a Recession
32. Effective Receivables Management in an Economic Downturn!
33. Real Estate & Property Sales Training
34. Credit Sales & Accounts Receivable Management

35. Selling Skills for Real Estate & Property Advisors
36. Take G.R.E.A.T. C.A.R.E!
37. Spa, Salon & Health Club Selling Skills
38. Selling Travel, Holiday & MICE Services
39. Selling Skills for Spa's, Salons & Health Clubs
40. Retailing in Salons & Spas
41. Selling Holiday, Vacation, Tours & Packages
42. The Power of Sales Referrals
43. Selling Luxury
44. Technical Selling Skills
45. Financial Advisors Sales Training
46. Dealing with Burnout at Work Monopolize Your Markets
47. Selling to Affluent Customers
48. Growing up with Grace
49. Financial Selling Skills
50. *The Effective Manager's Guide: Key Skills to Thrive*
51. From Aspiring to Inspiring: A Guide for New Managers on the Rise
52. The Power of Focus
53. Selling with Integrity: Sell Like Jesus The Perfect Role Model!
54. 31 Habits of Champions: Your 31-Day Journey to Greatness
55. Rejecting Grasshopper Talk: From Grasshopper to Giant-Killer-*Defeating Giants Daily!*
56. Navigate the AI-Powered Future of Bid & Proposals: Up-Skill to Stay Relevant with Alternative Career Paths & Opportunities
57. Hiring Sales Winners
58. Present with Impact
59. Success Unlocked: *Breaking Free from Habits that Hold You Back*
60. Complaints to Cheers, Feedback to Gold: Mastering Complaints Management
61. Thriving Together: *Cultivating Diversity, Equity, and Inclusion*
62. Coaching Skills for Sales Managers
63. Soaring to Success in Business & Leadership: Swifter, Higher, Stronger!
64. From Classroom to Podium: A Student's Guide to Powerful Public Speaking & Presentation Skills
65. Developing Self-Discipline
66. The CEO's 31-Day Power Plan: Unlocking Success through Essential Traits

67. Credibility Matters
68. A Winning Attitude
69. Bid & Proposal Management Using AI
70. Sales Forecasting: A Practical & Proven Guide to Strategic Sales Forecasting
71. Elevate & Energize: *50 Dynamic & Fun Activities for Peak Workplace Morale*
72. 'Sales SOS! Sales on Fire! *30 Days to Conquer Chaos & the Nightmares of Success!'*
73. Mastering Sales Managerial Skills: *Building High-Performing Teams & Driving Exceptional Results*
74. Eagle-Eyed Leadership: Unleashing the Power of 31 Lessons from Eagles
75. The Ultimate Employee Training Guide: *Training Today, Leading Tomorrow*
76. Being More Accountable at Work
77. Creating a Culture of Continuous Improvement
78. Effective Questioning & Listening Skills
79. The Power of Value Selling
80. The Growth Mindset
81. Mastering Professional Help Desk Skills
82. The Power to Lead with Empathy
83. Being Prepared: The Key to Unlocking Success
84. Youthful Spark-Youth Energizers, Activities and Games-Igniting the Fun in Youth
85. Ignite your Motivation for Success
86. Elevate Your Executive Presence: *Your Roadmap to Executive Excellence*
87. Smart Decisions: *Mastering Problem Solving with Strategic Solutions for Business Success*
88. Strategic Planning: *Developing and Implementing Strategic Plans to Achieve Long-Term Business Goals*
89. The Power of Stay Interviews
90. Developing G.R.I.T.
91. Adaptability
92. Diagnosis- *A Key Skill for Leadership*
93. The Burnout-Proof Salesperson: *The Master Guide to Preventing Stress & Burnout-* Strategies for Thriving in Sales
94. Learning from Failure: *Keys to Success*
95. Customer Success Management
96. Overcoming the Killers of Motivation
97. The C-Suite Code: *Mastering Skills for Executive Excellence'*

98. Dealing with Difficult Customers
99. Unlocking Your Potential: Mastering the Top 20 Life Skills for a Brighter Future
100. Nurturing Tomorrow's Leaders: *Essential Soft Skills Every Child Must Learn*
101. Lively & Fun Party Games for Seniors & Elders
102. Role Playing for Sales Champions: From Practice to Performance
103. Fun and Exciting Party Games for Kids
104. Case Studies for Sales
105. Role-Playing for Unbeatable Customer Service
106. Case Studies in Customer Service
107. Case Studies in Winning Negotiations
108. Case Studies in Management & Leadership
109. Case Studies in Human Resources & Talent Management
110. CEO Success Blueprint: The Essential Toolkit for CEOs and C-Level Executives
111. The Salesperson's Self-Coaching Guide: *Master Your Own Self-Coaching Plan for Success*
112. Overcoming Procrastination: *Your Ultimate Guide to Stop Delaying and Start Living Your Best Life*
113. When True Colors Are Exposed: *The Journey to Unmasking Humanity*
114. Life-Changing Habits for Teens: Teen Success Blueprint for a Bright Future
115. Workplace Stress-Free: *Proven Strategies to Thrive at Work and Beyond*
116. Objection Overruled: *The Ultimate Guide to Turning 'No' into 'Yes'*
117. Building Strong Teams: *A Comprehensive Guide to Team Building*
118. Ethical & Moral Leadership in Business: Eliminating Unethical Practices & Building a Culture of Trust & Integrity
119. Rising Strong: Building Positive: High Self-Esteem for a Fulfilling Life-*A Practical Guide for Students, Employees, Leaders & Entrepreneurs*
120 The Cheerful Mindset: Cultivating a Joyful Outlook Everyday
121. Leading Through Crisis: Case Studies on Crisis Management

From the Ministry side, Gerard graduated in the very first batch of Charis Bible College-India & had for over 9 years served as a Part-time Faculty at Charis Bible College-Chennai (Andrew Wommack Ministries-Colorado, USA). He also holds a Diploma in Worship (a subject closest to his heart) from the JSOW and is also a graduate of the Advanced Mentorship Program (AMP) and the Circle Of Ministerial Engagement (C.O.M.E.) of Prophet Jerome Fernando and a Spiritual Son of the Esteemed Prophet. An accomplished author of several Secular & Christian Books, Gerard has been on the board of a few international organizations and boasts of being the SON of the MOST HIGH GOD: An ordinary guy following an extraordinary GOD!

...And some of his most recent Christian Books being:

1. A Bouquet of Praises for My KING
2. Christian Jokes for the Serious Religious' Folks!
3. Jesus Healed You!
4. Praise24Ever! (also in Tamil version)
5. The 5G Network of GOD
6. Building Faith over F.E.A.R- FACE EVERYTHING AND RISE with JESUS
7. Hebrew and Greek Praise and Worship Words
8. Godly Mothers' and Grandmothers' Bible Story time for Kids!
9. Miracles of Jesus in Pictures
10. Raise your Praise all 365 Days
11. Thanking GOD with an Attitude of Gratitude
12. Meditating on the Attributes of GOD
13. Puppet Scripts
14. Alcohol Ruins, JESUS Reforms, Renews & Restores!
15. Habakkuk 2:2 Christian Daily Journal, Planner & Organizer
16. ABC of GOD's Word for Handwriting Practice
17. Daily Bible Verse Handwriting Practice (Building Godly Character & Faith through Cursive Handwriting Practice!)
18. Guiding Light: Fun & Faith-Building Bible Activities for Children
19. Rejecting Grasshopper Talk: From Grasshopper to Giant-Killer-*Defeating Giants Daily!*
20. Teen Titans of Faith: *Building Courage, Determination & Christ-like-Esteem*
21. I AM Empowered: *Unleashing Divine Power with Positive*

Declarations

22. Be A Solution Provider-*From Passion to Purpose*: *A Biblical Guide to Being the Answer to the World!*
23. Miracles of JESUS
24. Parables of Jesus for a Meaningful Life!
25. A Grateful Heart: Importance of Sharing Testimonies of GOD's Grace
26. Melodies of Worship to JESUS: 31 Songs of Praise & Worship From My Heart to HIS!
27. I AM SO BLESSED!
28. My Daily Cup of Energizer
29. 31 Leadership Lessons *from* Jesus- *The Supreme Leader*
30. Peace Amidst Storms: A Biblical Guide to Conquering S.T.R.E.S.S.
31. Rise Above: 20 Biblical Eagle Lessons for Life's Triumphs
32. Godly Goal Setting: *The FAITHFUL Blueprint for a Purpose-Driven Life*
33. The Profound Attributes of our Mighty GOD: Understanding the 10S's of the Almighty
34. Worship Now, Worship Forever: *A Journey from Earthly Praise to Eternal Glory*
35. Unceasing Praise & Worship: *365 Days to Worship the King*
36. The ROAR Within: *Living with Purpose and Authority through the Power of the Holy Spirit*
37. From Potential to Purpose: Unlocking and Multiplying Your Talents & Gifts for Kingdom Impact
38. Songs from the Heart: *Worshipping GOD in Your Own Tune & Melody*
39. Awakening Praise & Worship: Hebrew & Greek Words to Raise Your Praise
40. Sing a NEW Song to the LORD Everyday: *Daily Devotions of Praise & Worship to Lift Your Heart & Glorify HIS Name*
41. *The* A.R.O.M.A. of True Worship: *Creating Worship That Delights God*
42. Becoming A Kingdom Champion: *Embracing God's Call for a Life of Purpose & Victory*
43. The Busy Businessman's Daily Devotional: 366 Crisp Truths to Start Your Day Strong
44. The Teacher's Heart: *Daily Devotions for Educators*
45. Anchored! *A 31-Day Devotional for Students Facing Life's Challenges*
46. Suddenly! Unlocking Unorthodox Breakthroughs through Unusual Worship

47. Overcoming Adversity: *Lessons from the Bible for Modern Challenges*
48. LORD, Don't do it without me
49. Kingdom Leadership: *Biblical Principles for Modern Leaders*
50. Heartprints of God- *Growing God's Way:* Daily Devotions for Kids to Shine Bright
51. Send Judah First: Let your Praises Go up First to See the Mighty Move of GOD
52. DIVINE MOMENTS: *Recognizing, Embracing, Preparing, and Walking into Life-Changing Encounters with God*
53. Be a Builder in the Kingdom: *The C.E.M.E.N.T. Guide to Creating a Lasting Legacy*
54. Unshakable: *Pillars of Godly Womanhood* (Pillars of Faith That Changed History)
55. Lead Like a Shepherd: *14 Essential Traits for Pastoral Excellence*
56. The Worship Leader's Arsenal: *Powerful Exhortations to Ignite Thanksgiving, Praise & Worship*
57. Women of UnShakable Faith: *31-Day Devotional for Strength, Purpose & Influence*
58. Called to Teach: *A Complete 10-Week Training Guide for Impactful VBS Teachers*
59. Strumming for the KING: Cowboy Songs of Faith & Fire
60. The Ultimate Youth Camp Playbook: *50 Bible-Centered Indoor Games to Engage, Equip, and Empower Teens*
61. Glad in HIS Presence: *David's Revelation of GOD's Love & Mercy*
62. The Spirit Behind the Sound: *52 Devotionals for Worship Teams*
63. THE COWBOY'S COMPASS: *Riding the Trail of Faith with Grit & Grace*
64. Worship as My Weapon: *Living Victoriously through the Power of Praise*
65. A Worshipper Always Wins: *Living a Life of Victorious Worship*
66. Worship That Leads to the Throne: *Practical Strategies for Worship Leaders to Inspire Their Team & Usher People into God's Presence*
67. Worship as Warfare: *Conquering through the Sound of Surrender*
68. Watchmen on the Walls: *A 31-Day Devotional for Worship Teams*

69. KINGDOM BUSINESS: *52 Biblical Principles for GODLY Leadership & Wise Decisions*
70. From Evening to Morning: *Rediscovering GOD's Sacred Hours*
71. Waves of Glory: *Worship through Dance, Flags, Staff & Sound*
72. WORSHIP TEAM BUILDER: *Guiding Your Team from Formation to Fruitfulness*
73. The Worship Leader's Master Training Manual
74. Skits for the King: Children's Plays for Every Church Occasion
75. Unbreakable: Building Strong Marriages and Families God's Way *(From Vows to Victory)*
76. Songs for my King: *A 31-Day Journey of Praise*
77. Building Powerful Children: *Raising a Generation That Will Shape the Future for God*
78. Character Before Chords: *The Heart of the True Worshipper*
79. 365 Days Before His Throne: A Worshipper's Daily Declarations
80. Broken to Built: *How GOD Restores Lives, Heals Hearts & Uses Broken People for HIS Glory*

Besides regularly contributing to business & trade journals, including international ones such as the 'Creative Training Techniques' and the 'Sales News' of the U.S.A, He is also a member of several prestigious bodies & trade associations, having participated in many Conferences & Workshops in India & Overseas.

Prior to his last assignment of leading & managing a large MNC as head, Gerard had a 3-year stint in the Middle East as a Consultant with a leading British Consultancy Firm.

As the past 'Official Country Representative' for the International Business Award- 'THE STEVIES'-(the business world's own Oscar) for about 4 years- he ensured a few Indian companies that qualify for the same every year!

Gerard can be contacted at:

Email: training@Sales-Training.in,training@CollectionSkills.com
Websites:

- www.Sales-Training.in
- www.EtiquetteWorks.in
- www.CollectionSkills.com
- www.RetailSalesTraining.in
- www.SalesTrainingIndia.com
- www.ManualPreparation.com
- www.TrainingWithPuppets.com
- www.FirstContactAcademy.com
- www.SalesAndMarketingRecruiter.com

www.ingramcontent.com/pod-product-compliance
Lightning Source LLC
Chambersburg PA
CBHW062106160726
48282CB00026B/685
* 9 7 8 8 1 9 9 5 1 3 4 7 1 *